STEPHEN GRAY

with Trent Short

PLANTING
Fast-growing
CHURCHES

St. Charles, IL 60174
1-800-253-4276

Published by ChurchSmart Resources

We are an evangelical Christian publisher committed to producing excellent products at affordable prices to help church leaders accomplish effective ministry in the areas of Church planting, Church growth, Church renewal and Leadership development.

For a free catalog of our resources call 1-800-253-4276.
Visit us at: www.churchsmart.com

Cover design by: Julie Becker

© Copyright 2007

ISBN#: 1-889638-69-2

PLANTING
Fast-growing
CHURCHES

Table of
CONTENTS

Acknowledgements

I WANT TO THANK MY SAVIOR JESUS for the privilege of allowing me to be involved in a project like this. To God be all the glory!

To my wife and children: Marlene, I love you. Thank you for supporting me in everything. I wouldn't be where I am today if God had not placed you in my life. Ashley, Jennifer, and Rebecca, your prayers, encouragement, and patience throughout many long days of studying meant a great deal to me.

To Jack Connell, Ron Crandall, Leslie Andrews, Judy Seitz, Milton Lowe and the entire Doctoral staff of Asbury Theological Seminary, thank you for guiding me through this process.

Foreword

by Ed Stetzer

THROUGHOUT HISTORY, people have learned by oral tradition and from the stories of others. For centuries, workers' skills and crafts were refined primarily by learning from others' success and failure. Today, however, this practice appears to be less common, particularly in Christian ministries like church planting.

It seems like everyone is a church-planting expert nowadays. Many are making pronouncements about what works and what doesn't; few are doing the work necessary to confirm their assumptions. Church-planting books are being cranked out like romance novels—lots of promises and passion, but few facts on what does and what doesn't help church plants succeed.

While common sense and intuition are often accurate, sometimes they are not. And while scientific data and the cold, hard facts are often helpful when predicting future performance, they are also fallible. However, common sense that is also backed by scientific research is a valuable resource, and a gift to those whose everyday work can be helped by the insight it provides. This is what Stephen Gray has given us in this title.

Testing Common Assumptions

In this book, Gray tests the soundness of many commonly-held church-planting strategies and theories by surveying plants from around the country and analyzing the significant differences between those that struggle and those that thrive. The results of this report offer an array of rich findings for church planters, planting coaches and denominational leaders, who should find in it encouragement and helpful information, as well as a few warnings.

Church planters should be encouraged that many of Gray's findings support the conventional wisdom about church planting. For example, the study found that church planters who had strong emotional support, personal investment and conceptual freedom were more likely to succeed than those who had weaker support, investment or freedom. The research should also push planters to more and better preparation, as it confirms the effectiveness of those who allot time to raise their own support and maintain relationships with coaches or other supportive figures.

Warnings to Note

The findings should also come as a warning to some—cautioning against three particular errors in planting. When we plant in a hurry, without freedom of vision, or with a poor funding system, we are more likely to fail.

The first error is haste, when the plant launches and consequently struggles because of insufficient planning or resources. These planters may have launched the plant too early, before the time was ripe and the necessary funding, staff or core group members had been gathered.

Birthing a church is like birthing a baby—certain systems must be in place for it to be successful. A premature baby may not survive if he or she is born too early, and, if they do survive, their development tends to take longer. So it is with successful church plants; a healthy birth requires the right amount of time for preparation and development.

The second error consists of planting a church with a top-heavy, agenda-driven structure. The study's results reveal that leaders who have little conceptual freedom are more likely to struggle. This might be a plant from a large church that is led by a pastor (or denomination, network, etc.) with a very specific, recognizable personality and ministry emphasis. Although not willing to invest themselves personally, the "overseers" are happy to throw money at the plant—so long as it remains faithful to the likeness of the mother church. Gray's study shows that these "clones" tend to have a very poor life expectancy.

The third error deals with finances. Gray has again reminded us that planting a new church requires much more than just financial investment. Church planters need to pay close attention to this finding: The churches that received more funding for longer periods of time were overall less effective than churches that received less funding for shorter periods of time.

Granted, money can be a major factor in getting a church off the ground or getting the word out. But, when it comes to building an effective church, in the long run it appears that too much money has the reverse effect. A significant number of the successful new churches in Gray's study became mostly self-supporting within the first 6 months of their launch.

Listen and Heed

So where do we go from here? "Listen, listen, listen!" the Proverbs repeat, reminding our prone-to-wander ears of the rewards of wisdom. When attempting a work as important to the Kingdom as church planting, this advice is essential. Gray's report is a significant addition to the conversation about church-planting strategies and, if the planter is prepared to accept it, a new tool to help church planters plant more and better churches.

It is not often that you get the advice of 112 church plants, with clear results from some that are thriving and some that are struggling. So, seize the opportunity provided by this unique book.

You will be encouraged as you read this book. If you haven't planted a church yet, let this study soak in; you have much to learn, but don't ever lose the teachable spirit you have right now. If you are a seasoned church planter, you may be challenged to think a little differently about the types of churches you create. Either way, consider this an oral history of lessons learned, passed on to you through this book.

Preface

The Call

It was a cold January day, and I was staring out my office window at the winter-frosted trees. I was supposed to be writing a sermon, but instead I found myself day dreaming about the amazing things God was going to do through my church during the new year. I also found myself floating through the previous six years of ministering to this humble yet thriving Nebraska church. God had blessed us and moved in mighty ways. This small church had tripled its size and was beginning to burst at the seams. We had started a buzzing little daycare that was reaching out to over forty-five families. We had successfully transitioned one of our Sunday morning services into a more updated, upbeat, and contemporary affair. God had drawn over sixty-five people into a first-time relationship with Christ. And if that wasn't enough, we had also started a new Hispanic church, and it had taken off like wildfire. In its first year alone, we witnessed over fifty first-time conversions from this baby church. I stared out the window, distracted and smiling. How could God bless us more?

Yet, in the pit of my stomach, an uneasy feeling gnawed at me.

Everything seemed perfect—everything except this feeling in my gut. God's "still small voice" was speaking, telling me that He had something more in store for me. Most pastors would be overjoyed with my situation. Most pastors might look from left to right and decide to stay on course, but this feeling gnawed away at me, and I knew something wasn't quite right. *More?* I wondered. *What more could God have for me than this?*

"Well God," I muttered, "what are you trying to tell me?" God's voice didn't thunder through my office. Instead, the uneasy feeling remained. I stood, stretched, and decided the best way to discover what God was trying to tell me was to spend some time in prayer.

I suppose this sounds like a natural reaction for any good Bible-believing Christian. I suppose you're thinking, "Wouldn't any pastor stricken with a weird feeling in his gut pray to God for guidance?" I suppose that's a fair assumption…unless you know me. I'm a goal-oriented, task-driven person who doesn't do "slow" very well. Therefore, the idea of spending time alone, sitting still, waiting upon God's voice and possibly a slow revelation, was not appealing to me.

But I love God, and though waiting upon the Lord is not a natural act for me, I resolved to spend the next seven days in prayer and fasting. Perhaps this would speed up God's voice; perhaps God might grant me guidance beyond my sense of unease. Instinctively, I knew this week would be dangerous. God's calling is usually fraught with risk, and my intuition was telling me that God was about to ask me for a change. If God wanted me to make drastic changes in my church, I would make them. I was willing to do whatever God might ask.

After three days of prayer and ice water, God gave me a definitive answer. I had just walked into my house, and the phone rang.

"Hello?" I answered.

"Good afternoon, Steve. Do you have some time to talk?" It was David, and I did have time since ice water was the only thing on the menu. David was my conference superintendent and my respected friend, someone to whom I always enjoyed talking.

After the usual conversational formalities, questions about each other's families, and a quick volley of church and conference news, David came to the crux of his telephone call. He hesitated for a moment, and I knew I was in trouble.

"You know, Steve…I've been thinking."

I listened patiently as David tried to explain what God, over the last few weeks, had been communicating to him. In short, David had felt God guiding his thoughts toward church expansion. Understand, every church denomination is called to spread the gospel, which necessitates growth. A church might build a new, larger sanctuary or lay down a greater parking lot. This can be considered expansion, but this isn't what David was hedging at.

David came to the point: "Over the last couple weeks, God has laid a burden over my heart. I believe that our denomination needs to move, to grow, more aggressively than it has in the recent past. I guess what I'm talking about here is church planting. I've been praying about it and researching it, and it's a real financial risk. And as I've been contemplating and praying about this matter…"

My stomach clenched a bit. This was it. This was the change shooting through the phone like a flash of lightning.

"And Steve…" he hesitated. "Have you ever thought about becoming a church planter?"

One thunderous thought rumbled through my skull and up to God: "You've got to be kidding!" I wasn't mad; I just felt blindsided. Starting a new church had been the farthest thing from my mind. Why would I think of leaving? I had a church—a good church—which I had worked long and hard to nourish and guide into this bright new era.

After composing myself a bit, I related to David that I had been feeling God's urging to draw closer to Him for guidance. I told him that I was in the middle of a week of prayer for that reason. I also admitted that I had sensed that God wanted me to accept a new challenge or a change, but church planting hadn't ever entered my mind. I swallowed hard. I felt uncertain.

"Hey David?"

"Yes Steve?"

"Would it be alright if I called you back at the end of the week?"

"Sure, Steve," he said, "You take your time. I realize what I'm proposing would shake your life up a bit. You finish your time with God—that would be best—and then get back to me."

I would love to tell you that, having heard God's voice on the phone, having had my calling explicitly laid out for me, I immediately signed on the dotted line. I would really like to relate, on this page, that I packed up my family without a doubt or a question in my mind and headed for a new mission field…but I didn't. In reality, I resisted this blatant call. I had been searching for a new direction for my present ministry. I had been sniffing around for new ground to break. I didn't want a brand new calling. I didn't want to leave the party. I didn't want to start over, to build from the ground up. I didn't want to hand my thriving and hard-earned church over to someone else. And what if this someone else blew it? What if all I had grown here went to seed? What if I did it and failed? No, this idea wasn't what God wanted. It couldn't be.

Looking back on it, I think I knew right away that God was calling me to church planting. But the suggestion that I should leave my beloved church made me angry. I tossed and turned in my bed at night trying to understand why God would suggest such a silly thing. Sadly, I had become like any one of those guys in the Bible who were called by God to do something that didn't make sense to them.

"Hey Jonah," God said, "Why don't you go to Nineveh and tell those people that really hate you that I love them." Huh?

"Hey Gideon," God said, "Why don't you gather an army to go to war for me." And when Gideon finally does, God says, "Okay, now send most of them home." Huh?

And God was saying to me, "Hey Steve, why don't you walk away from a thriving community of new believers that we worked so hard to build." Huh?

It didn't make sense, and that made me anxious. I had no idea what a church planter did, and I wasn't sure I wanted to find out. Eventually I bought the only book about church planting that I could find, *Planting Growing Churches* by Aubrey Malphurs.

I sat down to read and quickly found myself enthralled by this book. I couldn't put it down. Malphurs emphasizes a growing need for new American churches, particularly in reaching the unsaved. He writes about how today's churches are stagnating, shrinking, and dying. Malphurs then draws his readers back to the Scriptures and reemphasizes the importance of the work of the Great Commission. In response, my heart began beating faster. My hands gripped the sides of the book, and I actually wept for the unsaved strangers and neighbors in my community. He brought their final judgment and their eternal fate and laid it at my feet. I felt a need to step forward. I felt a perfect need to tell the lost that Jesus loves them. I experienced a reawakening passion, a breaking heart for the lost, and a reshaping of my personal calling.

There was more to be discovered. I laughed nervously as Malphurs described the typical personality traits found in most church planters. I finally understood why, in my third year of college, I was told that I would never be a very good pastor. I was told that I didn't fit the typical pastoral mold. My personality tests described me as someone low on compassion, high on energy, long on ideas, and somewhat radical in my approach. These tests didn't lie, and I don't deny their truth. As a result, most of my career as a pastor I've felt like the proverbial square peg trying to fit into the round hole. I've always pushed the envelope, always question why we do things in certain ways. I'm the guy continually irritating my supervisors with questions, strange ideas, and suggestions involving change. These personality traits kept me feeling awkward in my role as a pastor, but this book, this wonderful book finally explained me to myself. "You're not weird," it insisted, "you're a church planter."

During my previous sixteen years of ministry the Lord had used me to transition three different congregations. The challenge was always the same. I was met with a struggling, stubbornly traditional, dying congregation, and I led this group toward a more open and outreach-oriented mind-set. In hindsight, I know that God had used these three churches and the experience I had gathered to prepare me for the next stage of my ministry.

I called David the next day and volunteered to plant a new church.

CHAPTER 1

School of HARD KNOCKS

CHURCH PLANTING REMINDS ME of the Indiana Jones movies. Every plant is a new adventure full of excitement and potential doom. Indiana was always chasing the elusive prize and never knew what pitfalls he would face around the next corner. Nevertheless, he pushed ahead and faced each problem in a new and creative way.

Remember the scene in the third movie where Indiana was standing on the side of a cliff looking across to the other side of a deep chasm? In order to get to the other side, find the Holy Grail, and save his father, he had to take a leap of faith. He didn't know that a hidden bridge would catch his fall and provide safe passage to the other side. Church planting is a lot like that dramatic moment. To do it, you have to take a wildly dangerous leap of faith. Church planting is the most exciting, the most frustrating, and the most brutal ministry anyone can do. It's exciting because it involves attempting something big for God. It's the most frustrating and brutal because it will test every area of your life. Church planters have to be dreamers, visionaries, planners, and like Indiana, they have to have nerves of steel and thick skin.

Church planting will make you feel alive, and it can push you to the brink of insanity. It will give you a new sense of God's presence and convince you that Satan is alive and well. You will celebrate the birth of a new church with unearthly joy, and experience betrayal from friends and family in ways you never thought possible. As a church planter, you will experience high highs and low lows. It's dangerous and dramatic. As they say on television—kids, don't try this at home.

After sixteen years of pastoral ministry, God called me into the arena of church planting. God called me, Stephen Gray, a skewed and flawed individual. What kind of a guy am I? I'm one of those driven individuals. I don't just like to win; I like to dominate. My little ducks not only stand in rows—they need to be smiling and looking directly into the camera. I've been diagnosed as a type "A" personality along with a very useful case of Attention Deficit Hyperactive Disorder. And God called me?

My preparation for this new adventure was both difficult and frustrating. As I prepared, I quickly discovered that church planting was not a very refined process. A multitude of varying models, philosophies, and conflicting opinions existed under the umbrella of church planting. With confidence and authority, each expert offered his or her opinion about the process, and every seminar or book led in a different direction. In a short time, the whole church-planting idea became overwhelming. I felt like writing these expert names on a dartboard, putting on a blindfold, and chucking a few darts. In truth, all of the books, the seminars, and the opinions were helpful, but none of them actually prepared me for my church-planting experience.

I spent an entire year gearing up for a move to central Missouri. During this year, because of my studies and research, because of my personal interaction with some of these experts in the church-planting field, I was convinced that within a short time, my future church would become the next great mega-church. I just knew I had what it took to "Git-R-Done!"

When I got to Missouri, I hit the ground running. I gathered a small core group of believers, as well as unbelievers, established a place of worship, and advertised my little church's opening. I threw all my energy and heart into this plant, and tried to remain hopeful. At the first preview service, one of the services we held before we officially opened, we had more than seventy unrefined, unsaved, and skeptical people. It was exciting! I had been blessed with the opportunity to lead these people on a journey towards Jesus. On that first Sunday, we were the third largest church in the district, and we hadn't even launched our public services yet. We were expecting to launch in three months with over two hundred attendees. Sad to say, it didn't happen. After that preview service things started to unravel. My family and I experienced a backlash of suspicion from the other pastors and lay people in the district. To top that, our denominational funding was going to be cut short; "After all," I was told, "you have enough people to support the church now."

One year later, my church plant was only attracting about seventy-five attendees per Sunday, and it was quickly losing momentum. A continuous conveyer belt of problems delivered obstacle after obstacle before my church. Money became a major source of frustration. The church had bills to pay and this left little funding for anything that might bring new faces through my doors. My focus shifted from growth to survival. As a result, the church stopped growing, and those that were attending regularly were feeling a sense of boredom. My church had plateaued after one short year; the whole church, myself included, had lost its sense of excitement and focus.

Things went from bad to worse when I realized my supervisor and I did not share the same church-planting philosophy. As a consequence, conflict began to build, funding of the church plant ended, and I was left to struggle alone. My wife and I had spent all of our savings and maxed out our credit cards because we believed that the district would come through for us. I was left alone to plant a church with only my personal wits and resources—which isn't saying much! We were left friendless, financially bankrupt, and demoralized. But I didn't care; with them or without them, I was going to plant a church. I knew God had called me.

God had a plan.

I wish I could say that I dug down deep and came up with a genius idea that saved this little church. I wish I could say that I prayed to God and He sent a hundred wealthy and generous visitors into my church the next Sunday. I wish I didn't have to admit that I did what many pastors do in the midst of ministerial difficulties: I began to question my calling and cast blame. I agonized while watching other church plants in the area flourish. One nearby church plant had launched on the very same day as mine, and it had gained an average weekly attendance of close to two hundred people. My church plant had fallen so far below my expectations.

I experienced many nights when I just couldn't go to bed. I would pace before a muted television set, reviewing the decisions I had made during the previous year. I had followed the advice of my mentor, and used the latest church-planting materials. I had taken advantage of every opportunity that presented itself.

This mental checklist, though I went through it compulsively, wasn't saving my vision of a thriving and dynamic church. Even though I had studied and made the proper church-planting preparations, my dream was quickly withering.

At this point, many career pastors simply walk away from the pulpit. And make no mistake, I felt like walking away. I was humiliated, demoralized, and confused. God, from my limited and mortal point of view, had led me out into a desert and then abandoned me. My denomination had removed all support from me and turned its back. I felt a sense of loneliness I had never felt before.

I was at one of the lowest and darkest crossroads of my life. I had entered into the school of hard knocks. But in the midst of this personal abyss, God was there—right there with me. He had a plan, and this was part of it. God knows me. He knows every fiber in me. He knows my every reaction before every circumstance. He knew that this barren and lowering experience would bear fruit in me.

Throughout this process, a pastor from another denomination and now a close friend, Dean Trivett, had been one of my prayer partners. He watched me weep and agonize over all my difficulties. He introduced me to the church-planting director of the General Baptist Denomination and, to make a long story short, they asked me to join their movement. They came rushing in like the long-awaited cavalry in one of those old black and white war movies. No, my little church didn't burst into the next great megachurch, but my financial worries ended, and more importantly, my original church-planting philosophy was taken seriously. The church grew steadily over the next year and then God introduced another surprise. I found myself elevated in status. Only in the sovereignty of God could anything like this ever happen. I was offered, and accepted, a position within my new denominational family as the Director of Church Planting.

Even though I felt that angels from heaven had swooped down and carried me away to a safer place, this dark experience left me with a sense of failure and a burning desire to uncover the factors that had led my church plant to stagnation. I spent hours poring over my processes and strategies. I had used the same techniques as the church plants that had grown rapidly. I had the "right mix" of spiritual gifts, the "right" church-planting personality, and a bold vision of what God could do. I had successfully transitioned three churches, and, with the help of a pastor from Mexico, had already planted a very successful Hispanic church. My failure didn't make sense, and this defiance of logic was a source of mental pain to me. "Why," I asked myself repeatedly, "had my church plant struggled, while others under similar circumstances were able to thrive and grow their attendances to a desirable two hundred or more within three years?"

This experience haunted me, and, I soon discovered I was not the only would-be church planter to have gone through this meat grinder. After many conversations with other church planters, I came to realize that my failure was not particular to me. In fact, these conversations seemed to paint failure as the church-planting norm! I learned that many church plants never grow beyond an average of eighty in attendance.

These long, question-filled sessions with other church planters sparked a strange hope in me and spurred a personal quest for a solution. This book is the product of that quest. It is my hope that the lessons I learned will encourage other church planters.

Though the drive behind my research is personal, the questions I seek to wrestle with are not. If I had to define my purpose in one sentence, it would be to reveal those factors that differentiate fast-growing, dynamic church plants from slower-growing, struggling church plants.

CHAPTER 2

Why Is Planting
SO IMPORTANT?

LET ME PREFACE EVERYTHING I am about to say with this firm conviction. The local church is the only hope for our world. The Church is not a human invention, simply a man-made organization created to oppress and control the people of the world. It is a divine, God-ordained, Christ-commissioned organism created to be an extension of the work of Jesus Christ. Its purpose is to offer salvation, wholeness, healing, and transformation to a sin-sick world. The local church is the only hope humanity has of finding forgiveness and proper standing before a holy and righteous God. Without the Church, the world has no hope. If you don't believe that, then there is no use in planting any churches. Close shop, go home, and forget you ever considered planting a church in the first place.

Throughout his ministry, Jesus exemplified the importance of evangelism. He spoke boldly and truthfully of the Father wherever he traveled. As his time on earth came to a close, he laid out the next phase of his ministry. The Great Commission, in Matthew 28:19, was his call to the Church to participate in the practice of evangelism: "Go and make disciples of all nations." Just before his ascension, Jesus reiterated these words. "But you will receive power when the Holy Spirit comes on you; and you will be my witnesses in Jerusalem, and in all Judea and Samaria, and to the ends of the earth" (Acts 1:8 NIV). The Great Commission was to be understood as a call to start new communities of believers wherever the disciples traveled.

Any serious reader of the Bible will quickly see that "God's nature is at the root of mission. The living God portrayed in the Bible is a sending God. He sends because of his love for the world."[1] The Church is called to be the living expression of the kingdom of God on this earth. It is to reach out to the lost with the truth and reality of the Gospel. It is to form loving, nurturing communities of new believers. In so doing, the Church, through the power of the Holy Spirit, should heal the spiritually sick.

The Great Commission is not a new calling to God's people. It goes back to the era of Genesis where God gave a very similar commission to Abram:

> *Leave your country, your people and your father's household and go to the land I will show you. I will make you a great nation and I will bless you; I will make your name great, and you will be a blessing. I will bless those who bless you and whoever curses you I will curse; and all the peoples on earth will be blessed through you. (Gen. 12:1-3)*

This call to Abram shows God's desire for Israel to become a movement that would touch the entire world, not merely a regional organization. God's desire was to bless "all the peoples on the earth" through Abram. God's design for the future of Abram's race is one that was intended to transcend the socio-economic and ethnic borders of Israel. Abram's obedience to God, after many generations, transforms itself into a nation of Israelites. This same obedience, taken on by Jesus' disciples, will again transform itself into today's Christian. God intended from the beginning—his call to Abram—for his Spirit to flow out of that nation into every nation on the earth. Israel, the nation that grew out of Abram's lineage, was to be the prototype of the Church. Genesis 12:1-3 stands as the foundation upon which the Great Commission rests.

According to the New Testament, God's children are no longer confined or defined by blood, or lineage to Abram. Rather, true Israelites are understood to be those who received adoption into the family through the blood of Jesus. "It is not the natural children who are God's children, but it is the children of the promise who are regarded as Abraham's offspring" (Rom. 9:8 NIV). Those who are followers of Jesus Christ and are a part of his Church are now, through their obedience to the Holy Spirit, transformed into the "children" of Abraham. This classification becomes significant, as followers understand that the Great Commission is a reaffirmation of the original call given to Abraham. The Church, like Israel, is not to become a stand-alone organization, but a life-giving organism that can influence the world.

Church planting is not new to denominational bodies. Church planting is and always has been the "intentional pursuit of lost people"[2] that naturally flows out of the Great Commission. As the Church involves itself in this work, it is fulfilling the original call, given to Abram, to be a blessing to all the people on the earth. Church planting, then, is a fulfillment of that call.

Many New Testament Scriptures, especially the book of Acts, can be used to show the importance of church planting. Acts offers the reader an up-close and uncompromising witness to the actions of the early Church. Acts presents itself as an important dynamic because it best illustrates the struggles and triumphs of believers actively pursuing the ideals of the Great Commission. In essence, it is the history of the first church-planting movement. Although the phrase "church planting" is not explicitly mentioned in Acts, I believe that the creation of new bodies of believers is implicitly understood as a "normal expression of New Testament Missiology."[3] If building and stabilizing new bodies of believers is church planting, then church planting was, without question, at the center of early Church activity.

On the day of Pentecost, God made it possible for the Holy Spirit to overflow beyond the borders of Israel. Acts 2:5 tells us that on the day of Pentecost, "God-fearing Jews from every nation under heaven" were staying in Jerusalem for the Passover celebrations (NIV). God's timing allowed for travelers to be present, ones who would carry the gospel back to their homes and begin local bodies of believers within their own communities. The varied groups of geographic origins present during the Passover celebration become a significant factor as one considers the rapid spread of the gospel. On that day, three thousand people "accepted his message [and] were baptized" (Acts 2:41). Peter's message and the subsequent conversions mark the beginning point of the momentum that would bring about the birth of the Church. The impact of that day reached beyond the walls of Jerusalem; it became a region-wide event.

The ministry, propelled like a rocket from Jerusalem, spread rapidly. The Christian movement quickly spread throughout all Jerusalem, Antioch, and the surrounding regions. By the sixth chapter of Acts, the good news of Christ's message had already spread northwesterly into Greece. Acts 6:1 tells that "the Grecian Jews complained against the Hebraic Jews." Sure, they're complaining, but amazingly, they've heard and received the good news.

Then, in his providence, God used the arrest and death of Stephen as an impetus for further expansion. Saul's brutal campaign to destroy the Church led to the very public stoning of Stephen, making him the Christian movement's first martyr. In turn, this bloodshed and Saul's oppressive tactics solidified faith and resolve among the new believers, and this recipe served to accelerate the Church's growth beyond Jerusalem. "If these early Christians had all stayed in one place, the gospel would not have spread nearly as rapidly as it did."[4] However, when discussing the persecution of the early believers, it should be noted that this persecution was not the only cause of a church-planting movement. The new believers did not swell their numbers in order to survive, fight back, or form a communal system of protection. Even before

Saul started his campaign against this budding movement, creating new bodies of believers had already been established as the normal mode of spreading the gospel.

After Saul's conversion, "the church throughout Judea, Galilee and Samaria enjoyed a time of peace" (Acts 9:31). The Church's rapid development underscores the fact that persecution did not cause the Church to move into the surrounding regions for the sake of survival; rather, the Church had already existed in these areas before Saul began his bloody campaign. Therefore, the church-planting movement in Acts should not be viewed as a reactive outcome of the persecution but a normal and expected outcome of the evangelistic call given by Jesus.

Even Saul couldn't escape the outpouring of the Holy Spirit. On the road to Damascus, he was confronted and converted by Jesus himself. Saul repented, changed his name to Paul, and quickly became the primary driving force for the Christian movement. Paul, driven and ambitious as he was, later set out on three missionary journeys. His vision was to plant and establish as many churches as he could in every city that would accept the gospel. Of these missions, Paul states, "It has always been my ambition to preach the gospel where Christ was not known, so that I would not be building on someone else's foundation" (Rom 15:20 NIV). Paul's statement reveals that his desire was not to build on another's work but to start new works.

Paul was a true missionary, and he acted as a nomadic and insatiable church planter. While history gives no clear understanding of how many churches Paul began through his three missionary journeys, the book of Acts reveals church planting as Paul's standard mode of operation. He moved from place to place establishing new bodies of believers wherever he went. And after leaving these new converts, he didn't forget them. He responded to news about each church's development by sending many personalized letters filled with love, encouragement, discipline, and constructive criticism.

However, the book of Acts covers more than the work of Paul. Peter made two missionary journeys of his own, and the remaining disciples spread the gospel across the surrounding regions. Acts is filled with numerous evidences of a church-planting movement in the early Church.

I believe God's design for his people—both the Israelites in the Old Testament and the believers in the New Testament—is for them to become world influencers. Both were given to a great commission. The believers in the book of Acts understood Jesus' Great Commission as a call to spread the gospel to every city and every region. The fulfillment of that calling was executed through the planting of new communities of believers. Church planting became a natural and practical expression of the Great Commission.

Why is it important to recognize and understand this early church-planting movement? Because the culture we live in would have you believe that the Church is nothing more than a human organization. Many modern Americans believe that you don't need to participate in your local church to be a Christian. The belief that Christianity is purely individual and personal is an exclusively Western concept yet pastors have allowed individuals outside as well as inside the church to believe this falsehood. In contrast, the early believers understood that Christianity was to be lived out within the context of a like-minded community. Like the early believers, we should understand, theologically, that it is not possible to be a Christian outside the context of a local body of believers.

While Jesus did die upon the cross for the sins of the individual, it is theologically incomplete to end the discussion there. Jesus' sacrifice was also for his Church. Paul states in Ephesians 5:25-27,

> *"Husbands, love your wives, just as Christ loved the church and gave himself up for her to make her holy, cleansing her by the washing with water through the word, and to present her to himself as a radiant church, without stain or wrinkle or any other blemish, but holy and blameless."*

Jesus died for the cleansing of future bodies of believers. His blood was shed for you and me, but it was also shed to cover his beloved bride, the Church.

Without local bodies of believers, without the community of the church, the individual Christian will not be interconnected, supported, or able to live out his or her life as God intended.

Sadly, the latest report on church attendance in the United States shows that only 17.5 percent of the American population attends church on a given Sunday.[5] In this report, David Olsen also points out that the American population has grown, while the total number of churches in America has actually declined. According to the Association of Religious Data Archives, there are only 139,791 evangelical churches in the United States. With the American population topping the 300 million mark, that means there is one church for every 2,200 people.[6] This suggests that even if every American wanted to go to church on Sunday morning, there would not be enough seats to hold them. If we believe that people need the Church, then we can only come to one conclusion: we need more churches!

CHAPTER 3

Hitting the 200 MARK

A CHURCH PLANT IS A LOT LIKE A BOULDER on a barren mountainside. You've seen this same rock in many adventure movies. Perhaps you've seen two nondescript cowboys desperately prying it loose, and then watching it fall. It quickly picks up speed, knocking other smaller rocks loose. Rocks smash against other rocks, breaking them from their resting places. All at once, a clamorous noise ensues, dust rises, and suddenly the entire mountainside is alive with the violent motion of falling boulders and debris. This landslide is what the cowboys were hoping for, and they whoop and holler at their success. A successful church plant is a lot like this scene.

For this study I focused on church plants, that, like a rolling boulder, generated enough momentum to reach an average weekly attendance of 200 within the first three years of public launch. I could have used any number, but conventional wisdom among most church growth experts is that this barrier is a significant momentum shifter in the life of a church. Steve Sjogren, an expert among church planters, writes, "With fewer than 200 people, a church will need to fight just to stay alive. With fewer than that number of people, you will not have hit your stride. It is inevitable that your attention will be focused upon trying to maintain the basics of church survival."[1] According to Peter C. Wagner, a church plant should "expect to pass through the 200 barrier within about twelve months after going public. If you are not through it in two years, something is going wrong and your chances of ever doing it are greatly diminished."[2] A church plant that hits this mark quickly will be thrust forward with momentum and will have a greater possibility of retaining a growth pattern.

So, just how quickly should a church plant expect to reach 200? Some say it should happen in the first year; others believe you should reach it within the first 18 months. What I discovered was that both times are valid, but the "magic" cut-off time, if you can call it that, was closer to twenty-four months.

According to the data, 77 percent of the fast-growing church plants involved in this study reached an average weekly attendance of 200 by the twenty-four-month mark. Only 23 percent of these fast-growing churches broke the 200 barrier after that time. It is statistically significant to understand that if a church plant has not broken this barrier within the first two years, it increases the likelihood that it never will.

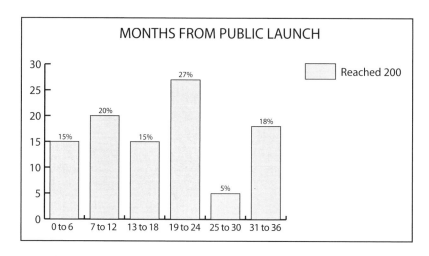

The graph above shows that only 15 percent of these fast-growing plants reached 200 within the first six months, 20 percent reached 200 by the end of the first year, and an additional 15 percent reached 200 by the end of eighteen months. This is revealing because many in the church-planting world believe that if a church plant doesn't reach 200 within the first eighteen months, it probably never will. But statistically, only 50 percent of these plants reached 200 within that time frame.

The largest grouping, percentage wise, was between months 19 and 24. A total of 27 percent of these church plants reached 200 within this time frame. Combining the percentages so far reveals that somewhere between 19 and 24 months is the real cut-off point. If a church plant does not reach and exceed 200 attendees within the first two years, it has only a 23 percent chance of doing so.

Momentum is a major issue that either works for or against the church plant. If all goes well, a small, excited group will reach out to their neighbors and invite them to join their new church. The invited, in turn, invite their neighbors, and so on. Hopefully a spiritual avalanche will form. But unlike the movie avalanche, and more realistically, the boulder rolls, hits a few other rocks, kicks up some dust, and bounds lonely and recklessly into the chasm without making the desired impact.

Momentum is not something with which only church plants struggle. Many established churches lack a sense of momentum. Recent research reveals that "80 percent of all churches have fewer than 200 worshippers on Sunday Morning."[3] This research also shows that the average American church numbers around seventy-five attendees on Sunday morning. Amazingly, many of the struggling church plants examined in this study fell perfectly in line with this statistic. I would speculate that these plants also experience the same survival problems as the average American church.

The 200 barrier is a critical marker in the life of any church. A church plant that doesn't hit that mark quickly is likely to become just another statistic. It will be like the reckless, futile boulder that comes to rest at the bottom of the canyon. It stands to reason that the quicker a church plant gathers a critical mass of attendees, the greater the momentum it will gain. This critical mass will help the young church avoid the difficulties intrinsically tied to limited attendance numbers. If a church plant can reach and break through the 200 barrier quickly, it has a greater chance of beginning a spiritual avalanche.

The importance of reaching an average attendance of 200 should not be underestimated. There is strength in numbers. Evangelism, outreach, and servicing the needs of the infant church can be much easier if there is a larger crowd from which to draw workers. "Generally speaking, pastors of larger churches have come to feel that they can get the job of evangelism and Christian nurture done better than pastors of small churches."[4] If a church plant can reach and break the 200 barrier quickly it can become a potent source of evangelism, and experience a rate of conversion at an accelerated pace.

Carl George and Warren Bird write in *How to Break Growth Barriers,* "This figure [200] is not an exact or magical number (the range is actually between 150 and 350), but it does represent a critical growth limiter that the vast majority of churches hit."[5] Many experts, including Bill Sullivan, Steve Sjogren, Lyle Schaller, and Peter Wagner agree with and have added to the collective wisdom surrounding the 200 barrier.

Every organization experiences critical tipping points at which it either gains or loses its ability to move forward with any momentum.[6] This tipping point has been experienced in multiple settings throughout history and is recognized as the "rule of 150."[7] The rule states that once a group grows beyond 150, it will begin to take on a different structure and feel. Groups above 150 will need more than one leader in order to keep them focused and growing. For example, most churches above this number will need an associate pastor or a group of active leaders to help with general facilitation. Groups under 150 are more easily controlled and led by a single individual.

While 200 may not be a magical number, I believe it is absolutely imperative to find and keep the momentum necessary to carry the church plant through to the next level. Scientists understand that the formula for momentum is mass multiplied by velocity. The mass of any given entity, when set in motion, has a bearing on the momentum that propels it forward. The greater the mass, the greater the momentum will be. The same holds true in birthing a new church. This concept is commonly referred to as building "critical mass." Once reached, this critical mass is harder to stop and easier to keep in motion.

I admit, however, that the correct size of a church is relative to its contextual setting. A church of seventy-five may seem quite large in a small town or rural setting. It may even be a very effective congregation, given their circumstances. On the other hand, a church that has maintained a consistent attendance of seventy-five, in a metropolitan setting is, most likely, stagnant and ingrown.

The size of a congregation will, by and large, set the agenda for its future viability and effectiveness. Please understand, I am not questioning the commitment and call of church plants that do not reach the 200 mark quickly. I am simply stating what twenty years of experience has taught me: that unless a church plant hits the 200 mark quickly, ministry is slowed, and the danger of falling into survival mode is greatly increased.

The Small Church Problem

Too often small churches struggle to grow. A main reason for this is that small churches, while effective in some ways, tend to be very close-knit and do not allow visitors to feel at home as readily. Lyle Schaller refers to churches under the two hundred mark as "Collie" churches: "Some people tend to wonder why these churches remain on a plateau in size or why church shoppers often do not return after that initial visit. Collies tend to have strong affection for members of the family, but they often bark at strangers."[8] When any church falls into this mode of operation, growth becomes almost impossible. Myriads of books and articles have been written about the growth problems of the small church. The key to avoiding this problem altogether is for a new church to reach the two hundred mark quickly. New church plants that do not grow rapidly will develop a "Collie" mentality, stifling their ability to reach out and impact the community. Planting new churches should be an attempt to overcome growth problems, not emulate them.

A church in the city which never reaches the 200 barrier could have a very limited ministry future. Why? Because 200 "is the minimum number of adults needed, in a metropolitan setting, to provide the services people want in a church."[9] A church plant is no exception. It, like all churches, will experience a plateau in its attendance. If the church plant experiences a plateau below 200, its effectiveness in delivering the gospel through multiple ministries will be severely hampered.

Ministry Options

We live in a culture that loves choices—in fact, we have come to expect choices. If you go into any convenience store looking for soda, how many choices do you expect to find at their fountain? Two? Unthinkable. Four? Probably not. I'm guessing, but I bet most have at least eight different spouts to choose from. The same idea of choice holds true in today's church. Once a church plant finds itself limited by low attendance and resources, it will inevitably be limited in what services it has to offer a community. Limited choices and services will make further church growth very difficult to accomplish. By contrast, if a church plant can reach the 200 mark quickly, it will be better able to provide multiple ministries quickly and avoid losing the momentum needed to continue effective ministry. So, if a new church isn't able to offer multiple ministry options quickly, it will find itself unable to compete with the myriad of already established churches that do.

To some degree, every church struggles with this problem, but the church plant is even more vulnerable. While an established church may be able to do adequate ministry with an average attendance of less than 200 over an extended period of time, a church plant cannot. Established churches have several advantages that baby churches do not.

Credibility

Most established churches have buildings that give them visibility. Established churches also have been able to build credibility over many years in their community. In some case, these older churches have become a community institution. They have a proven staying power and an accepted reputation a new church hasn't had time to build. Too often, church plants are viewed with suspicion and even labeled "cultish." Rapid growth of a new church can create enough "buzz" to help give it the credibility it needs.

Finances

Established churches have had time to build a loyal membership. Often, this loyal membership consists of extended families that have invested themselves in the history of the church. This loyalty creates a strong financial foundation. Members give because they have always given or because Mom and Dad gave. Conversely, a church plant rarely has the advantage of traditional and institutionalized tithe. A church plant almost always starts out with a small number of attendees and is thus limited by their financial resources. The acquisition of basic things like tables, chairs, sound systems, and computers, can become a huge financial burden for a church plant.

Corporate Esteem

Of all the problems that new churches experience, this may be the most difficult to overcome. Crowds attract crowds. Think about the last time you were in an unfamiliar town and needed to choose a restaurant at which to eat. Didn't a part of your selection process include counting the number of cars in each parking lot? I bet you turned to your spouse and said something like, "Wow, that barbeque joint sure is busy. I bet they're good." Whether you realized it or not, you were attracted to the size of the crowd, not sign or building's façade.

To create new missions that break out of the mold of the self-serving, survival-minded, family-run organizations, leaders must find a way to plant churches that can pack out their pews and parking lots in a very short period of time. Growing rapidly increases momentum because it fosters a healthy attitude among members. "A primary difference between growing and declining churches is their attitude. Growing churches feel they have something worthwhile to offer to their community. Their high level of self-esteem provides the energy and strength to share the gospel of Christ with people in the community."[10]

Church plants that do not grow beyond the 200 average attendance mark within a few years will lose momentum and fall into the small-church trap that will result in a low sense of congregational morale. Church plants are infused with a heightened expectation for success. Very often, these new congregants are driven by a desire to change the world. This desire and the high expectations make church plants vulnerable. When a churchgoer's experience is not met with immediate success, discouragement can set in. This can be a fatal blow for a young church.

The members involved in an established church usually have fairly reasonable expectations. Most have settled into a routine way of "doing" church.

Members may pray for, expect, and hope for growth, but the level of expectation for dramatic and rapid changes is not as high as in a new church. In contrast, the expectation of those involved in a church plant should be one of rapid growth within a short period of time. When expectations are not reached at the level anticipated, a sense of failure is certain.

Once an attitude of defeat settles into the hearts and minds of the church planter and the new congregation, they can very easily begin to view themselves as "small, weak, unattractive, powerless and frustrated with a limited future."[11] Unfortunately, this attitude is the state in which many church plants find themselves. If conventional wisdom is true, two-thirds of church-planting attempts will begin to develop a small-church self-image. The bottom line is that church plants need to reach the 200 mark quickly or face a myriad of problems.

Good Is Not Good Enough

Church planting is a tough and brutal business, and many church plants quietly pass away. Of the church plants that do survive, many simply mimic the problems of the average American church, and others, like mine, experience a loss of momentum and decline. "Most church plants start too quickly and they end up settling in to be a church of 75 to 150."[12] Once a church reaches this level of stagnation and decline, its ability to refocus toward growth and ministry is severely limited.

According to George Barna's research, "the typical experience seems to be that, once a church loses its momentum, the most probable outcome is either death or stabilization at a much smaller size."[13] No church planter or leader sets out to start a shrinking and struggling church, but many end up in that situation. Every denomination hopes to impact this nation with the gospel of Jesus Christ, and all church planters dream of planting a fast-growing, dynamic church. I know I did. I wanted to be the catalyst behind the next great megachurch.

The drive to fulfill the Great Commission propelled the modern Church into its present place in society. The Holy Spirit spread his work across our nation's geography and history, and many were converted. Churches sprang up. One doesn't have to walk far in any town or city to find the churches this movement built. But look inside them on any given Sunday morning. Is growth and excitement the norm? Perhaps some are growing, but as a whole, statistics about church growth paint a picture of stagnation and decline.

Many denominational leaders are facing up to this serious problem and planning for the future. When facing the possible outcome of simply ignoring the problem, many church leaders are prayerfully asking: "How will we survive and thrive beyond this present decline, and maintain our drive to share the gospel?" Over and over again these leaders are answering this question by planting new churches.

I believe they are right to do so. In order to stem this tide of stagnation, we must begin planting churches to which people will flock. We must differentiate between the great young churches and the ones that merely exist. In his book *Good to Great*, Jim Collins gives us a simply stated proverb for the modern church: "Good is the enemy of great."[14] Thom Rainer's book, *Breakout Churches*, supports that statement with this little gem; "It is a sin to be good if God has called us to be great."[15] This "greatness" mentality should be followed in church planting for two reasons.

First, denominations are spending millions of dollars each year on their church-planting programs with meager results. Strangely, many church leaders seem comfortable planting sub-standard churches. That may seem like a bold statement, but the fact is, of the 2,285 church plants that qualified for this study, only 168 of them had reached 200 within a three-year period. Most of them ended up mirroring the average size of established churches (sixty-five to eighty) in America. We have to be wise stewards of the resources God has given us to manage. Jesus' parable of the talents in Matthew 25 is a perfect example. He closes out the story by saying, For everyone who has will be given more, and he will have an abundance. Whoever does not have, even what he has will be taken from him. (NIV) As a denominational leader, I feel the pressure of the eyes watching me to make sure I am using the people's generous donations in a proper, effective and excellent way.

Second, and more important, the way we plant a church can have just as strong of a negative effect as it can a positive one on the people who choose to attend. A poorly planned church might create negative experiences that could sour new converts and their future views of Christianity. A well-planned and booming young church will feed, encourage, and enthuse the new convert into a lifelong walk with Jesus. The eternal destiny of our friends, family, neighbors, and co-workers depends on our ability to share the gospel in a compelling way to a desperate and needy humanity. Church planting is a major requisite of sharing that saving Gospel. It is far too important to leave up to speculation and wishful thinking.

CHAPTER 4

Research SPECIFICS

Driving Questions

My intention in writing this book has been to reveal common ingredients found among dynamic church plants, ingredients that are lacking in the less-than-stellar comparison church plants. My hope is that the discoveries found in this research will enable church planters, denominations, and other sponsoring agencies to have a better understanding of extraordinary church plants.

What makes this particular research project different from other studies on church plants is the intentional separation of the two distinct groups. My focus has not been to identify why a church plant remains open or closes; rather, it has been to identify specific differences between ordinary church plants and those that have clearly become extraordinary.

Most agree that a church plant will rise or fall according to its leadership. But leadership is only one factor. Should the church planter carry all the blame for a struggling or anemic church? Or are church planters made to be scapegoats when other factors contribute to a church plant's failure? Through my conversations with other church planters, denominational leaders, and heads of church-planting departments, I developed a questionnaire that addressed forty-three different issues involved in church plants. (A copy of this questionnaire can be found in the appendix of this book.) This questionnaire was designed to answer three basic questions:

1. Does the personality of the church planter play a part in the growth of the church?

The personality of the church planter is considered a major contributing factor in determining whether a new church becomes and remains viable. Church planters are often portrayed as extroverted, visionary, proven leaders who are able to handle adversity. Each church planter must have the ability to develop and employ a strategic plan for a new church. He or she must also be able to sell the vision to others and create solidarity among those who follow.

I used Dr. Charles Ridley's Assessment developed for testing church planters' personalities to discover the level of leadership ability of each participating church planter. This assessment is utilized by many denominations in varying forms. I will discuss this assessment more in chapter five, which deals with leadership ability.

My intention was not to discover whether or not the individual was indeed a church planter. I wanted to find out if the church planter's assessment score had any bearing on whether or not his church plant reached the fast-growing, dynamic status.

2. What role did the support of the sponsoring agent play in determining whether a church plant became dynamic or struggled?

Too often, planters and leaders think of support only in terms of money. But support is so much more than throwing dollars at a church. In order to create a healthy new-church environment, support should cover at least four areas: finances, freedom to create, emotional support, and church-planting training.

How a denomination or sponsoring agency utilizes these areas of support will have an effect on the growth and viability of the church.

3. Are there any differences in the methods used between fast-growing church plants and struggling church plants?

In the first year of a new church's existence, every planter is faced with countless decisions, from the mundane to the important—where they will plant, whom they will target, what kind of facility they will use, and many more. The answers they give to those questions have a lasting impact on the development of the church plant. Two crucial decisions that the planter must make deal with the method used to build the core group and the pre-launch strategy. This third question was designed to determine the impact of differing methods used by a church plant and to discover how these methods factored into the growth of the church.

Participants

All church plants and planters involved in this study were part of a denomination or larger sponsoring body. In order to qualify for this study a church plant had to meet three criteria.

First, in order to have an up-to-date, relevant study, I didn't want to include older church plants. So, all church plants had to be at least three years old and no older than six. Times have changed and the lost change along with social currents. Therefore, I wanted to have the freshest data possible.

Second, all church plants had to have been led by a first-time church planter. Most church planters are novices to this specialized mission field. Those who have planted and returned to the field have already learned and experienced the "do's" and "don'ts." If I had included this group, it could have skewed my data.

Third, all church plants had to be planted within a city of at least thirty thousand people. Planting a church in a rural setting is very different and, in some ways, even more specialized than the urban setting. Many churches in rural settings will never reach or surpass the 200 barrier. Because the lower population density will not allow for it. In fact, in some rural settings a church of 125 might be considered a megachurch. It wouldn't make sense to compare more metropolitan church plants to those in an urban setting.

Once a church plant qualified, it was placed into one of two groups: fast growing or struggling. In order to qualify as a fast-growing church plant, the church had to have reached both financial self-support and an average attendance of 200 within three years of its public launch. By contrast, a struggling church plant may have met one of these qualifiers, but was not able to reach both within the three-year time limit.

A total of 2,285 church plants within five denominations qualified for this study. I was amazed to discover that only 168, or 7 percent, of the 2,285 qualifying church plants were able to be counted as fast growing. While many people tell tales of fast-growing, dynamic church plants, they seem to be the exception and not the rule. In fact, only 7 percent of the church plants, within these five denominations, over a three-to six-year period were able to accomplish self-support and 200 in average attendance. I believe we can safely extrapolate that percentage to church planting as a whole, which means that 93 percent of church-planting attempts will not reach 200 in average attendance and run the risk of settling into a possibly crippling average within the first three years of existence, or die altogether.

This study will provide you, the reader, with information on the key factors involved in fast-growing church plants, and hopefully give you the ability to raise the percentage of probability for planting a fast-growing church.

Gathering the Information

Since the struggling group was much larger than the fast-growing group, I created a comparison group of equal size—168 of the struggling church plants by random selection. The total sample size was, therefore, 336 church plants.

On January 7, 2007, I sent out 336 questionnaires to the church plants invited to participate in this study. Of the bulk sent out, 131 questionnaires were eventually filled out and sent back to me, making this study's participation rate 38.9 percent.

The fast-growing, dynamic church group filled out and returned 79 of the 131 questionnaires, a 60.3 percent participation rate. As I examined their data, I had to disqualify eighteen of these seventy-nine responses. Even though these eighteen were considered fast growing by the prospective leaders, they did not meet the full criteria of the fast-growing church plant set out by this study. In the end, I was actually able to move three of these disqualified surveys into the struggling church group to make use of their data. So data from a total of sixty fast-growing church plants was recorded for this study.

The struggling church plants filled out and returned 52 of the 131 questionnaires, a 30.9 percent participation rate. However, one was disqualified, and two were moved to the fast-growing group because they were self-supporting and had reached the 200 mark. In the end, data from fifty-two struggling church plants was recorded for the study.

Finding Significance

So, how did I determine if a finding was significant or not? That's a pretty good question, and it's one that I had to ask a statistician. I might be fairly competent handling numbers, but I've never claimed to be a math geek. I do, however, know how to get one on the phone. After a few baffling conversations and a lot of questions asked, I finally understood how to declare a finding significant.

In order to avoid a long explanation, I will keep the following brief. The findings discovered through this study were measured using two different means.

First, three of the sections were measured using a statistical t-test showing differences between the mean averages of two groups. In the questionnaire, the questions dealing with conceptual freedom, personal support, and the church planter's Ridley Score used this method to discover significance. This will be further explained later.

Second, I used a simple percentage of difference to discover significance for the rest of the questions. According to the statistician I spoke with, anything above a 15 percent difference could be counted as significant.

Enlightenment

In March 2006, I began the journey to find the answers to my burning questions. Since then I have logged many hours of phone calls, e-mails, and letters. I have spent more than a few days locked in my room poring over data. If what I discovered would help only me, I felt I could finally get some closure, some sense of relief. Little did I understand the impact this research would have. What started out as a personal and somewhat selfish quest has turned out to be an exciting and motivating time of discovery. A total of twenty-one significant differences were discovered between fast-growing and struggling church plants. While many more questions were asked of each planter, only those differences which qualified as significant are in this book. You can find a brief overview of the other findings in the appendices of this book. If you desire a copy of the full study, e-mail a request to *fastgrowingchurchplants@ yahoo.com*.

My hope is that the discoveries made through this study will help planters, denominations, mother churches, and other sponsoring agencies plant strong, healthy churches. Thousands of attempts are made each year and only a few become truly fast-growing, dynamic churches. The following chapters will show you what these extraordinary church plants had in common.

CHAPTER 5

Leadership
ABILITY

THERE ARE ALL KINDS OF LEADERS and all kinds of leadership styles. There's the lead-by-example leader, the dictator, the persuader, the gifted orator, and the hands-on leader. But what kind of leader does it take to plant a fast-growing church? Before trying to come up with an answer on our own, let's listen to Paul as he addresses that question to the church in Corinth: *"And God has appointed these in the church: first apostles, second prophets, third teachers..."* (1 Cor. 12:28 NIV).

Let's examine this verse for a moment. Here, Paul himself is listing different groups of church leaders: apostles, prophets, and teachers. What's his point, and what's my point in drawing your attention to this verse? Very simply this: within his church, God gives different gifts to people to fulfill certain tasks. Notice how Paul has organized different leadership styles under vastly different categories. Beyond this, he even goes as far as to put them in a specific leadership order. In this brief verse, he lists his church leadership groups from the top rung of influence on down. Paul understood that different kinds of leaders existed within the Church and not all were called to be the top leader. In fact, he goes on to say that this leadership configuration is by God's design. Simply put, the Church will naturally foster many leaders, but most will not be called to be the one in the driver's seat.

This leads me to my point: when a leader tries to climb into a higher sphere of leadership influence, into an area he might not be designed for, he will hit a lid. In his book *The 21 Irrefutable Laws of Leadership*, John Maxwell opens with his "Law of the Lid." This law refers to an individual's maximum ability to lead effectively. You might be a natural leader, but everyone who leads has a ceiling or limit, to their leadership ability. Using two scales of one to ten, each measuring leadership and leadership effectiveness, John Maxwell explains it this way:

> "If your leadership rates at an 8, then your effectiveness can never be greater than a 7. If your leadership is only a 4 then your effectiveness will be no higher than a 3. Your leadership ability—for better or for worse—always determines your effectiveness and the potential impact of your organization."[1]

This law is relevant to the realm of church planting. Not everyone who wants to be or claims to be a church planter *is* a church planter. Neither is every church planter able to lead a new church at the same level. Effective church planters are a very specially wired group of individuals. They are also a specifically called group. If God has not called you to be a church planter, you will not have a great deal of success in your church-planting attempts. You may be a good leader in some other ministry or business, but if God has not specifically called you and empowered you to plant a church, don't even think about it.

Within the arena of church planting, there are some who are better designed to lead than others. Not everyone is called or wired to be a Bill Hybels, Rick Warren, Ed Young Jr., or Troy Grambling. Although many aspire to those heights, most will not reach them.

I have defended many church planters as they were being sacrificed on the altar of success—my heart goes out to them. However, like every other good researcher covering this topic, I must assert that leadership is a crucial element in the development of a church plant. One person's ability to lead can make or break a church plant. It's a fact that some people are endowed with greater leadership skills than others. The real meat of the issue is this: is there a significant difference between the leadership ability of church planters who lead fast-growing church plants and those who lead struggling church plants? How do a planter's personal characteristics affect his ability to plant a fast-growing church? I did not seek to discover whether or not these leaders were qualified planters; rather, I sought to discover if there was a difference in the level of their leadership ability.

In 1984, Dr. Charles Ridley, a professor of psychology at Indiana University, conducted a study of church planters involving thirteen different denominations, providing him with forty-eight different characteristics of church planters. Of these forty-eight characteristics he listed thirteen as essential and they have become the standard for assessing church planters. These thirteen characteristics can be found in *How to Select Church Planters* by Dr. Charles Ridley, and they are:

1. Visioning capacity
2. Intrinsically motivated
3. Creates ownership of ministry
4. Relates to the unchurched
5. Spousal cooperation
6. Effectively builds relationships
7. Committed to church growth
8. Responsive to community
9. Utilizes giftedness of others
10. Flexible and adaptable
11. Builds group cohesiveness
12. Resilience
13. Exercises faith[2]

Each planter taking this test was asked a series of questions designed to display and measure these thirteen characteristics. Each question used a scale of 1 to 5, with 1 (Strongly Disagree) as the low and 5 (Strongly Agree) as the high. After the test was taken, the numeric answer for each question was totaled and averaged according to the number of questions asked. The higher the average, the greater likelihood an individual had the characteristics necessary to plant a church.

The research questionnaire sent to qualifying planters asked them to give their Ridley Assessment score, if they had taken the test. Of the one hundred and twelve planters that responded, eighty-five revealed their Ridley score. Forty-seven of those who gave their score were leading fast-growing church plants, and thirty-eight respondents were leading struggling church plants.

The results were surprising. On average, the planters leading fast-growing church plants scored significantly higher than those who were leading struggling church plants. Those leading fast-growing church plants scored an average of 4.26 out of a possible 5. Those leading struggling church plants scored an average of 3.82. While the margin may initially seem small, after running a standard statistical t-test on the scores of those who participated, the finding easily qualified as a significant difference. According to this statistical test, anything below a difference of .05 is considered significant. A .000 difference was discovered between these two groups of church plants making this a significant find.

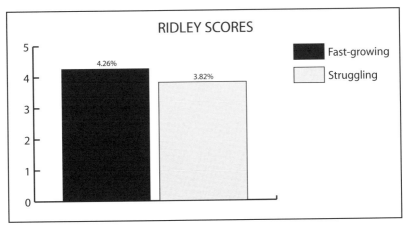

This finding is significant because the higher a potential planter scores on this church-planting assessment, the greater possibility he has of planting a fast-growing church. While this is only one piece of the puzzle, it's a big piece.

The success of a church plant has a lot to do with getting "the right people on the bus."[3] For me, this became more apparent when I compared the Ridley scores of the struggling church plant surveys against the fast-growing ones. This finding implies that a sponsoring agency wishing to plant a fast-growing, dynamic church plant should take the Ridley test, or any other proven assessment process, seriously.

Finding the highest quality church planter possible is a must if the goal is to plant a fast-growing church. Planters need to be able to cast a vision, and gather a core group of people around them who are excited enough to follow the vision. The right church planter will be internally motivated to raise additional funds, build a larger core group, and allow these people the freedom to add to the vision of the church. The higher the score on the Ridley, the greater capacity he or she will have to do these things.

One major caution must be mentioned here. A high score on the Ridley Assessment alone does not mean that a planter will be a super-planter. In fact, some of the planters who were leading fast-growing church plants did not fare much better than those leading struggling church plants. In several cases, planters of struggling church plants scored higher. While extremely important, the assessment score is only one factor among many. While a planter may have a high or low score on the assessment, he or she may still fail due to an absence of other factors.

Now let's take a look at one of these other factors needed for a fast-growing, dynamic church plant: money.

CHAPTER 6

Too Much or
TOO LITTLE

THE AMOUNT OF MONEY IT TAKES to start a new church is always a sticky issue. When I was trying to start my church, I spent thousands of dollars on things like rent, promotion, equipment, the day-to-day bills, etc. And with every dollar spent, I felt torn. It seemed that I was throwing dollars at much-needed things, but I always needed more. And then, I felt embarrassment about this money pit while explaining my financial state to my superiors. I have heard countless individuals, planters and denominational leaders alike, complain about how expensive it is to start a new church.

Most pastors and congregations of already established churches take for granted their secure financial and material status. How easily we forget about those pioneers who started the church we worship in today. Those brave men and women who started the church we love and protect may no longer be alive to remind us of the enormous sacrifices they made. Big buildings, nice carpet, padded pews, stained glass windows, tables and chairs, and all the material things inside the local church were earned by the sweat and blood of our fore-fathers. We are so removed from these beginnings that we can't recognize the costs involved in starting a new church.

Let's not be shy about it: church planting is very expensive. If you are not willing to invest multiple thousands in a church plant, don't even begin. Remember the old adage, "You get what you pay for"? Whoever coined that phrase must have been a church planter. If you are a denominational leader and you want to start a new church by rubbing a couple of dimes together, remember, "You get what you pay for." The quickest way to kill a church plant, or at least doom it to a life of anemic survival, is to shortchange it.

On the other hand, if you are a church planter and you think that a denomination or sponsoring church should give you everything your heart desires, you're wrong as well. Too *much* money can also have a negative effect on a new church. Church plants are intended to become self-supporting as quickly as possible. Far too often, the cries from church planters for "More! More! More!" are answered with more, and the plant falls into a welfare pattern.

Church planting is, in many ways, like raising a child. You would never think of having a child and then not spending your money on her. The baby cries out with hunger pangs; you buy formula and feed her. The baby yawns, droops in your arms, and you supply her with a crib. You would naturally tend to her basic needs. As she grows and learns to walk and talk, however, she will begin to desire different things. But you don't give her everything she reaches for, do you? If you give a child everything she asks for, she becomes spoiled and dependent. A church plant is exactly like this. It will have many needs, but that doesn't mean a denomination or sponsoring agency should supply all those needs without question.

If a planter cannot bring a church to self-support within three years, this might mean that the wrong leader has been chosen. While I agree that it takes money to plant a church, if your chosen planter repetitively asks, "How much money do I get?" run! If the fire is in his belly, if the call has been branded on his heart, the planter will move forward regardless of what you give.

Between 1979 and 1984, Rudee Boan researched church plants in the Southern Baptist Convention. He discovered that little evidence existed in support of, "finances having any influence upon the outcome of a mission."[1] In fact, his research ultimately came to the conclusion that unsponsored churches were much more likely to become constituted. He also concluded that the proper use of finances was more important than the amount given. While I agree that proper use of finances is an important issue in the life of any church plant, good stewardship is difficult if the church does not start with a realistic amount of resources.

On the other hand, in 2000, Dennis Powell studied five different denominations and their church-planting practices. His research revealed that one difference between a church surviving or failing was "the level of funding available."[2] Powell's research also revealed that a new church's first three years of income are vitally linked to its becoming self-supporting. Powell summarizes this phenomenon:

By looking at total income available the first three years of a new church, those with total income above $30,000, including offerings, gifts, and subsidies, had a significant advantage. Those below $30,000 in total income each year became self-supporting at a rate of 23 percent. Those above the $30,000 threshold had a 77 percent rate of becoming self-supporting.[3]

Out of all the churches involved in Dennis Powell's study, only one reached the 200 mark in the first three years. This particular church had over 350 attendees by the end of the first year. However, the amount of financial support offered to that particular church is not mentioned.

Funding is extremely important in the life of a new congregation, and a "new church will require a regular flow of money."[4] To my knowledge, little research exists on the appropriate range of funding needed to start a new church. Financial support is a heavily debated topic among church planters and denominational leaders, and allocated resources are generally left up to those involved. The amount of finances often varies according to the model of church-planting employed. My research sought to discover an answer to this issue.

With all of that said, how much money should a church planter be given to start a new church? The questionnaire sent to each planter involved in this study had eight questions that would seek to discover the answer to this question. I discovered that there is a delicate balance between too much and too little.

Work Status

The first question in the survey was directed at the work status of the planter. Many church planters are required to supplement their personal income while planting a church. This means that they have to get a job and plant a church at the same time. So, my study sought to discover whether it is more beneficial for a church planter to be a full-time church planter or bi-vocational. My questionnaire asked each church planter about his or her work status as a planter. The data revealed that both the fast-growing and struggling groups had a high percentage of full-time church planters. However, the "fast-growing" church plant group had a 16.8 percent higher rate of full-time pastors than struggling church plants. Remember, the cut-off point is 15 percent. So, this is a significant difference.

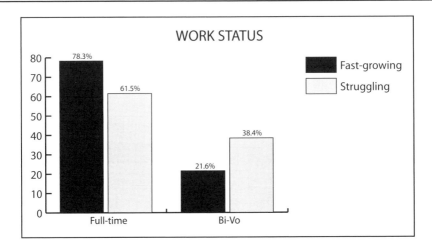

The fact that the majority of fast-growing church planters were full-time did not really surprise me. Imagine being in a new town, and having to look for a new job, perhaps at the hardware store or in an office setting. Then, after attaining a new position, imagine learning all that is required to effectively fit into this new routine. Then, on top of that, imagine going about the all too often discouraging business of starting up a new church in this new environment. It only makes sense that a person's ability to focus fully on the more important task at hand will lead to greater success. If a church planter is worried about earning a living, his attention is split, and he will have less ability to maintain an intense focus on the church plant. I don't think I'm assuming too much when I say, a planter's focus is absolutely vital during the early years of the church plant.

Years of Salary Support

Here is where things begin to get interesting. For the most part, planters of fast-growing churches were not given salary support beyond three years. No significant difference was discovered between the two church plant groups in the first year. But then, very few church plants were limited by only one year of financial support. However, in the second and fifth years, when financial support ended for church plants, significant differences were discovered. When a church plant's finances were cut off at the end of the second year of existence, there were 23.4 percent more fast-growing church plants than struggling ones. When a church plant's finances stopped at the end of the fifth year of existence, there were 25.5 percent more struggling churches than growing. These are both significant differences. Remember, I said that a delicate balance exists between too much and too little money. This finding begins to bring that to light.

To look at these findings in another way, of the fast-growing church plants, 91.2 percent received salary support for no more than three years. By contrast, of the struggling church plants, 77.6 percent received salary support for three or more years. This data would seem to imply that an extended period of support is detrimental to the development of a church plant.

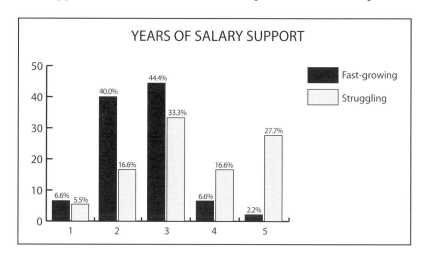

This finding may run counterintuitive, but a lengthier time of support had a negative effect on the church plant. A church planter who is given too much salary support over a long period of time, stands a better chance of falling into a slower growth pattern with less chance of becoming self-supporting. It may be that the promise of financial stability over a long period of time causes the planter to relax and even become a little lackadaisical. Think about it, if you know your salary is set and secure for the next five years, wouldn't you continually tell yourself, "No problem…I've still got time." If the planter knows that his salary is set for the next five years, he might not feel pressured to work very hard at helping the church to grow, nor will he be in a hurry to teach financial stewardship. A shorter period of financial support forces the planter to be aggressive in growing the church, raising additional funds, and teaching a proper, biblical understanding of financial stewardship.

So, how much should a full-time planter receive? How much salary is necessary over a two-to three-year period? I didn't study that aspect of the financial question. I believe it is safe to say, however, that a planter's salary should be commensurate with the area in which he is planting. A planter in the Midwestern United States will, more than likely, not need as much as someone going to New York. A planter should be paid enough of a salary to support his or her family.

Additional Start-up Money

I was also interested to discover a significant difference between fast-growing and struggling church plants as it concerned additional start-up money. Start-up money is additional funding beyond the planter's salary. This is money that is used exclusively for the new church and is usually spent at the discretion of the planter. Each planter was asked if he received any additional money beyond his salary, and if so, how much and over how long a period.

A significantly higher percentage of fast-growing church plants (26.9 percent) received financial support from their sponsoring agency beyond salary support.

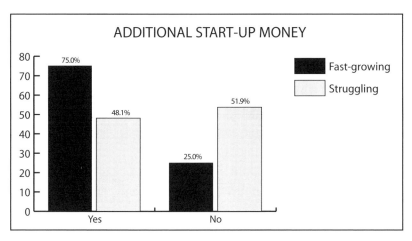

Again, this was not a surprise to me. Remember, it takes money to plant a church. It takes money to advertise the opening of a plant, to buy a sound system, to pay the rent, water, and electricity bills. It takes money—period. However, I was very surprised by the amounts of additional support given, as well as the time frames during which it was given.

Amount of Additional Support

According to the data, significant differences show up between the fast growing and struggling groups of church plants at the $10,001 to $25,000 range and at the over $100,000 range. Thirty-five point five percent of the fast-growing church plants only received between $10,001 to $25,000 in additional funding. By contrast, only 8 percent of the struggling church plants received this lower amount of funding. At this funding range, the difference between the fast growing and the struggling was a staggering 27.5 percent. Amazingly, this trend was almost the reverse for the over $100,000 range. Only 6.6 percent of the church plants that received over $100,000 of additional funding ended up qualifying as fast-growing. And unfortunately, a whopping 32 percent of the church plants that received over $100,000 of additional funding found themselves earning the struggling label. In the over $100,000 funding range, the significant difference between the struggling and the fast growing was 25.4 percent.

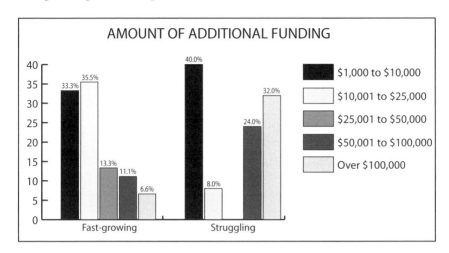

This delicate funding balance becomes very clear when looking at the above graph. Struggling church plants seemed to be on one end of the spectrum or the other. They received either too much or too little. By contrast, fast-growing church plants where found in the middle.

However it is interesting to note that, by in large, fast-growing church plants received far less additional start-up money than did struggling church plants. Another way of looking at this finding is to combine the first three support ranges and contrast them to the last two support ranges. A combined total of 44 percent of the struggling church plants received $50,000 or less additional funding. By comparison the vast majority (82 percent) of fast-growing church plants landed in this funding range. Likewise, a combined total of 56 percent of struggling church plants received over $50,000 in additional funding while only 18 percent of fast-growing church plants received this amount. The significant difference between the fast growing and struggling church plants in these combined ranges of additional support was a massive 38 percent. In this higher range of funding, more churches struggled than became fast growing.

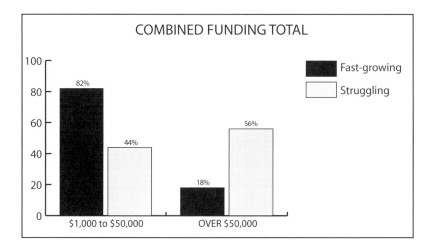

To me, these findings were very surprising. In essence, this shows that many denominations are pouring vast amounts of money into church plants in the hopes that they will somehow spring into life. Yet, at the same time, it also seems to be showing that this financial flow might be dowsing the very fervor it takes to create a new church. I say this because the higher percentage of fast growing churches clearly falls into the lower funding ranges.

Time Frame of Support

You might imagine that the church planter is brought into an office and his denominational leader writes a big fat check. "Here you go," he might say, "go plant yourself a church." Of course, this isn't the case. Financial support to the plant, in almost all cases, comes in increments. Since my research sought to examine the issue of additional support, in order to examine that more closely I felt it would be prudent to look also at the time frames in which these moneys were received.

According to the questionnaire results, a majority of fast-growing church plants (60 percent) received all of their additional funding within the first year. By contrast, only 38.4 percent of struggling church plants received the total of their additional funding within the first year. The difference between the fast growing and struggling church plants that received all of their funding during year one was 21.6 percent.

Of the church plants that received funding incrementally over a five-year span, only 2.2 percent were found to be fast-growing church plants. By contrast, 23 percent of struggling church plants received funding for a full five years. That's a difference of 20.8 percent.

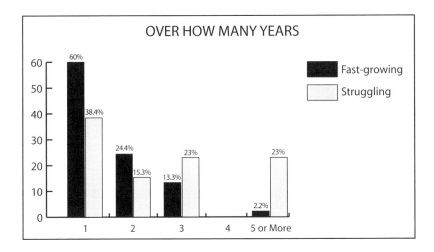

As with the previous question, the significance of this finding is amplified when combining and contrasting these five years. A significant number of fast-growing church plants (60 percent) received the total of their additional funding during the first year. And like a reflection in a mirror, the struggling church plants stand on the other side of year one. Over the remaining four years, 61.6 percent of struggling church plants, an almost equal percentage, received additional funding.

While a higher percentage of fast growing, dynamic church plants received more funding than their struggling counterparts, most received $25,000 or less within a one-year time frame. I would speculate that this indicates these plants were given a start-up grant. By contrast, struggling church plants that received additional funding received far more financial support over a longer time frame. In fact, a significant number of struggling church plants received over $50,000 over a four- or five-year period.

Again, it may be that giving too much money to a new church will cause it to fall into a welfare mentality, a mentality that becomes increasingly difficult to overcome. The highly funded church plant may begin to believe that the sponsoring agency that made the initial investment will also jump in and solve any financial problems they may have in the future. If they do come to believe that they have a wealthy sister church with big and generous pockets, they could very easily relax and disregard their own sense of financial responsibility.

Personal Involvement

The ability to fund a church should not rest entirely upon the agency sponsoring the plant. The planter should also be involved in raising financial support. After all, it's going to be their baby. Until this point in the questionnaire, every financial question had to do with a sponsoring agency's part. The questionnaire ended by addressing each planter's personal involvement in fund raising. The planter was asked if they had had to raise any additional funds beyond what was already being offered by the sponsoring agency.

When the results were tabulated, 63.3 percent of the planters of fast-growing churches indicated that they were personally involved in raising additional funds beyond what the sponsoring agency provided. Of the struggling church planters, only 23 percent indicated that they were personally involved in raising additional support. That's a difference of 40.3 percent.

It doesn't take a statistician to see that a significantly higher percentage of fast-growing church planters were personally involved in raising some of their own additional financial support than struggling church planters. I believe this finding reveals a correlation between a planter's sense of personal responsibility in fund raising and the success of his church plant.

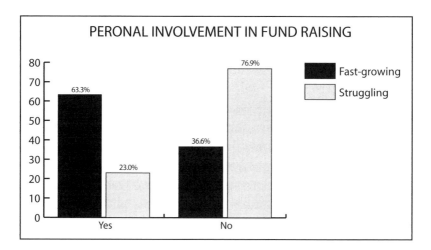

Conclusion

Several significant discoveries were unearthed while taking a good hard look into the financial differences between fast-growing and struggling church plants. I have discovered that most planters leading fast-growing church plants worked full-time as church planters. These full-time church planters earned a set salary package lasting no longer than three years, and the highest percentage of them had their salary ending at two years. Most planters leading fast-growing church plants were also given an additional financial package from a sponsoring agency of up to $25,000 over a short period of time. (The vast majority of these received the entirety of their funding during their first year.) These successful planters were also far more personally involved in raising additional support beyond what they received from the sponsoring agency.

By contrast, planters leading struggling church plants usually worked as bi-vocational planters. Most of these planters received salary support for three years or more. (Almost 45 percent of these struggling planters received salary support for four to five years.) Only about half of these planters received any additional funding from the sponsoring agency. However, of the 48.1 percent that did, these struggling churches received more than $50,000 over a longer period of time. These planters were also not very personally involved in the raising of any additional funds.

From this analysis we can form the ideal financial profile for a church planter. A church planter should be paid, for no more than two years, to do the work full-time with an amount that is commensurate with the average median income of the area in which he is planting. The planter should also receive somewhere between $25,000 and $50,000 in the form of a start-up grant and should be required to be personally involved in raising funds for the church plant.

Ultimately, I believe the amount needed to plant a fast-growing church will be somewhere within the $200,000 to $300,000 range within a two-year period. This amount will cover things like a salary for two full-time leaders, (I'll speak about that in chapter ten) rent, utilities, equipment, and curriculum for youth, children and adults. On top of this is the enormous cost a church plant must absorb in order to complete a strong marketing campaign.

Marketing is one area I did not study. However, I help the church plants I lead, to implement a marketing strategy that will cost thirty to forty thousand dollars—just to launch the first public service. Granted all of this is dependent upon the style of church you are planting.

CHAPTER 7

FREE to BE

IN ORDER TO START NEW CHURCHES, to start them from the ground up, we must be innovative in every part of our approach. According to Leonard Sweet, author of *Aqua Church*, "The church needs to employ its immense imaginal resources in the service of spiritual enrichment and betterment."[1] The church cannot continue to do business as usual if it expects to reach this new and differently wired generation. Television, computers, iPods, Internet, and video games have brought the American culture into a new era of communication and entertainment. "If we want to communicate, we will have to learn a new rhetoric."[2] Because of the rapid changes we have experienced, every established church and every church plant is forced to compete with these technological and cultural advances whether we like it or not. The church must adapt to this technologically savvy culture if it is to effectively fulfill the Great Commission. Either denominational leaders will frame the innovations employed during the creation of a new church, or this task will fall to the church planter.

The new church plant needs a plan, a good hearty strategy, prior to its launch. A map of immediate decisions outlining a proper church launch is vital to any plant's survivability. Control, within certain boundaries, is to be expected in any structure: "One challenge for a denomination is to allow appropriate freedom to the local church. The energy for church-planting does not emanate from a headquarters building."[3] Denominations usually invest, at some level, in the life of these new churches, so a level of accountability should be expected. But just what level of accountability is appropriate? How much freedom of initial church-planting decisions should be given to the church planter? What must be made clear is how the level of accountability exerted on a new church affects its growth.

Lyle Schaller believes control belongs mainly to the denomination because it has the proper resources available to design, organize, and implement a comprehensive plan for the plant.[4] The other side of the spectrum calls for leaders to give most of the control over to the planter. In his book *Church-planting: The Next Generation*, Kevin Mannioa makes some strong statements in favor of giving the church planter more freedom:

> Get out of their way. Ego may suffer when the realization suddenly hits that they do not need your expertise in order to function. They may know more and have more experience. It may simply be that they have it all together. For you to assume that they need your help may be a misplaced if not crippling assumption. Your greatest ministry may be to affirm them and stay out of the way. They are bright enough to call if they need help. Even at that, allow them the freedom to call someone else as a resource instead of you.[5]

I believe Mannioa is correct. Church planters in the field have a clear understanding of the needs of the community and how the new church can address those needs. They are the eyes and ears on the street. They hear the daily gripes and joys of their budding congregation. They are living it. An individual in a headquarters building is not as intimately connected to the community being served. Once the location is chosen and some initial demographics are completed, I believe the church planter should have full control.

In his research, Rudee Boan indicates that when a new church is dominated by the sponsoring agency, this master-servant relationship will "damage the mission with its paternalism."[6] My study attempted to discover if the control of a sponsoring agency has any bearing on whether or not a church becomes a fast-growing, dynamic church plant.

The survey sent to each planter asked a series of six questions having to do with control.

1. How much input did you have in creating the vision for the church?
2. How much input did you have in determining style of worship?
3. How much input did you have in hiring your own support staff?
4. How much input did you have in determining where the church was planted?
5. How much input did you have in determining your target audience?
6. How much input did you have in determining how the funding was spent?

After each question, the planters were asked to rate the amount of control they had over these basic decisions. Their answers were recorded on a Likert scale, in this case, a scale of one to five. A score of one to two represented that the planter believed the majority of control in this area had been exerted by the sponsoring agency. A score of three represented a balance of control between the sponsoring agency and the planter. And finally, a score of four or five represented an area where the planter felt as if the decisions or control of this area had been his own.

Three significant differences were discovered through their responses. Planters leading fast-growing churches indicated they experienced greater freedom in forming the vision for the church plant, a greater freedom in choosing their target audience, and greater freedom in determining how the funds of the church plant were spent.

As mentioned earlier in this book, several areas of my research used a statistical test to determine if the findings were significant. This statistical test is called a "t-test". It measures the means and standard deviation of the data collected. By comparing and contrasting the data from both groups, a value is determined to reveal significance. According to the "t-test" any value less than .05 is considered a significant difference. Of the six areas within conceptual freedom studied, three contained significant differences between fast-growing and struggling church plants: vision, target audience, and spending of funds.

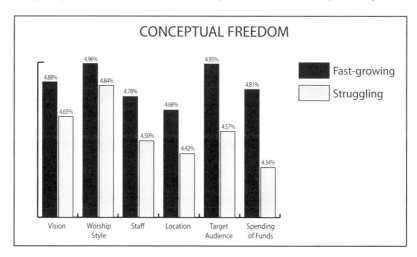

In my opinion, the freedom to make one's own choices on the mission field is vital. This is especially true when it comes to casting a vision for a church plant. The results plainly show that the church planter with control over his or her own church vision is much more likely to succeed. In the area of church vision, there was a significant difference between the fast-growing and struggling church plant groups.

The vision for a church plant must be birthed in the heart of the individual planting the church. When a sponsoring entity forms a vision, then asks someone else to fulfill it, there is a good chance the church plant will struggle.

A planter once told me that a denominational leader with a dream to plant a church had approached him. This leader mapped out the location: a fast-growing city located in the American Southwest. For years, this denominational leader had carried a heartfelt vision for this city. In response, the planter jumped on a plane, flew to the city, and immediately fell in love with the area. This man was a true church planter. He was called to plant and he loved a challenge. This planter had a deep and holy drive to follow the Great Commission. Yet, three years and $250,000 later, this church plant was struggling to survive, and it ultimately closed.

After asking this church planter a few questions, I soon discovered that even though the planter loved the idea at first, his joy soon faded. While the planter was a wonderful and capable leader, the vision for this plant wasn't birthed in his heart. Rather, it came from the heart of another, and he adopted it. This man had acted nobly and obediently; he believed he was doing God's will. But beware: if God isn't moving in the heart, if God isn't molding a personalized vision, wait! It's dangerous to force a preset vision on a church planter. Allowing the planter the appropriate freedom to respond to the vision God has birthed in his or her heart will create a greater possibility for a fast-growing church plant. I believe it is safe to say that leaving this conceptual freedom to the church planter will create a higher probability of planting a fast-growing, dynamic church, because there is greater personal ownership.

A natural outflow of the planter's church-planting vision is the choice of a target audience. For example, if the planter has a burden for young adults, this vision might include upbeat music and a casual approach. If the planter has a burden for farming or rural communities, this vision might include a lot of potlucks, outdoor sermons, and family-oriented activities. Imagine forcing a planter with a particular type of calling into an area or mission field that he or she is not excited about. The results are going to be substandard. So, I was not surprised to see that the freedom to choose the target audience was another significant factor. Planters leading fast-growing churches had far more freedom to choose the audience they would target for the plant.

Finally, planters leading fast-growing churches were also given more freedom to spend their funding in a way they saw fit. I believe this speaks to the idea of micro-management. No one knows better which resources are needed than the person in the field. If the congregation is continually complaining about the sound system that squeals and squawks for mysterious reasons, shouldn't the repairs or replacement of this item be up to the planter? If this planter was bright enough to gain a denomination's trust over a new church, shouldn't it be assumed that he is bright enough to make this decision? While every planter should expect the sponsoring agency to exert a certain amount of administrative control, I believe most of the financial decisions should be up to the planter.

In every category, the fast-growing, dynamic church plants averaged less control and/or management from the sponsoring agency. The survey's accumulated data indicate that sponsoring agencies need to give proper freedoms to church planters.

The planter should be given the opportunity to pray over and form the vision God has placed on his heart. It's hard to fulfill someone else's vision. If a planter can't articulate a vision, they shouldn't be allowed to plant. People follow vision and if the planter can't clearly share his vision, or if he is uncertain about a vision he hasn't birthed, then it will be hard to get others to follow.

The target audience of the planter will more than likely be reflected in the vision. If a planter envisions starting a contemporary service then the attendees will probably be younger in age. That age group, more often than not, reflects the age of the planter. While I am not suggesting a planter cannot cross generational barriers, I am suggesting cross generational church planting may take a special individual. A planter should have the freedom to choose the target audience God has placed on his heart.

Finally, a planter needs freedom to spend the funds as he sees fit. The planter is the one on the field and closest to the project. While sponsoring agencies should help a planter write out a good financial plan, no one can plan for every event. A planter should be trusted to use funds appropriately. If a sponsoring agency has to micro-manage a planter because he can't be trusted, they may need to reconsider planting a church with this particular planter.

CHAPTER 8

The Barnabus
FACTOR

HAVE YOU EVER STOPPED TO THINK what Paul's ministry might have been like without Barnabas? True, Paul was a driven man. Paul had go-go-go galore, and had he taken the church planter evaluation, he would have passed with flying colors. I'm sure, even without a guy like Barnabas next to him, he would have had a great impact on the culture, planted a few churches, and even enjoyed a time of measurable success. Yet I have to wonder; did Barnabas play a significant role in the success of Paul's ministry? I think so!

Paul needed Barnabas. Let me explain. By the time Paul was converted, he had a black reputation among the Jews. Paul, formerly known as Saul, was infamously known as a violent, hateful, murderous persecutor of those who followed Jesus. Where the blood of new converts was spilled, there was Saul, like a vicious predator, drinking in each death. Obviously he was good at ferreting out new believers, because everyone was afraid of him. As Saul, he was probably one of the most powerful Jewish leaders of his time. He describes himself as a Jew who was, "circumcised on the eighth day, of the people of Israel, of the tribe of Benjamin, a Hebrew of Hebrews; as to the law, a Pharisee; as to zeal, a persecutor of the church; as to righteousness under the law, blameless" (Phil. 3:5-6 ESV). Saul was no small player.

Suddenly, Saul is converted, and he is claiming that none other that Jesus himself saved him. I'm sure this far-fetched story was met with skepticism. I bet Jews and Gentiles alike thought Paul was going undercover to get to the kingpins behind this budding religious movement. The Christians of that day were suspicious of Paul. They realized that if they allowed him into their inner circles and he turned out to be an imposter, their lives and the lives of their families might be snuffed out in the middle of the night. Would you have trusted Paul? I'm not sure I would. At any rate, Scripture helps us to under-stand that he wasn't trusted. Most would have been quite comfortable to let Paul fend for himself.

Then there was Barnabas. Barnabas was involved in the new Church and had a good reputation among converts…and he accepted Paul. The Bible never allows us into this conversation or series of conversations between these two, but somehow Barnabas was able to believe in Paul's conversion. If it had not been for Barnabas's belief in Paul's intentions, it is likely Paul would have never been accepted into the ranks of the converts, given their stamp of approval, and sent on missionary journeys by the church in Antioch. Barnabas was the key Paul needed to enter into his new life's mission. God used Barnabas in a very important way. Barnabas's trust propelled Paul's ministry to a whole new level. Those who formerly distrusted Paul soon stood behind him, and like Barnabas, they too sought to elevate and support Paul's calling to go forth and spread the good news.

So what is my point? Church planters are often treated like Paul, begin-ning their new position as outsiders. As they go about the business of planting a new church, they are viewed with suspicion, seen as competitors, misun-derstood, and left to fend for themselves. In many ways, they have a tide of emotional stress that constantly threatens to pull them under. Too often, the personal and emotional support of a church planter is overlooked. The pattern of planting usually goes like this: "Here's your training. Got it? Good. Here's your money. Take care with that. Oh, here's how much freedom you have to shape your church with. Understand? Good. Okay buddy, go get 'em!" This all sounds good, but then the church planter goes out into the big bad world alone—alone with his mission, alone with the pack of emotional stresses just waiting to surround him.

Any ministry is lonely, but the nature of church planting amplifies this loneliness. Often, living in a new town with no friends, far from their spon-soring agency, many church planters feel isolated, detached, and misunder-stood. The added pressures involved in church-planting can elevate that sense of loneliness to an all-time high and can lead to burnout. Because of this, encouragement is a big issue among church planters. The level of emotional support a church planter receives from the sponsoring agency will play a huge part in the emotional well-being of the plant itself.

My first church-planting experience began with great hope and expec-tation, but it ended in failure. I was not prepared for what I would face on the field from my fellow pastors and ministers. I expected distrust from the unchurched in my new community, but I did not expect the animosity I faced from some of the religious leaders surrounding me. My surprise inflated dramatically as I dealt with the animosity directed at me from some colleagues in my own denomination. All of this unexpected disapproval weighed heavy on my heart and cast me into a state of depression. After my first year of church planting, I almost walked away from the ministry.

In 1984, the *Journal for Advent Christian Thought* published an article by John Roller about church-planting success and failures within the Advent Christian Church. Roller discovered that new Advent churches planted in an area that have more than thirteen other Advent churches have a "16% better survival rate" than new churches planted in an area with fewer than thirteen churches.[1] Roller attributes his findings to what he labels the "fellowship factor." Roller's study also found that church plants have a "19% better survival rate"[2] in states that attempt to plant more churches. His point is, the more attempts made by a given state, the more supportive, open, and accepting that group of churches are to church planting in their areas.

In 1995, Larry McCrary studied essential elements in church planting. His study was designed to look at relational issues involved in strong church plants. Out of this study, seventeen principles for starting strong new churches were developed. McCrary's fifth principle has to do with the personal and emotional support given by a sponsoring agency. McCrary reveals that emotional support from a sponsoring agency is vital to the health and well-being of both the church planter as well as the plant.[3]

In my own experience, I found that handling the ridicule and resentment from my own group added almost intolerable levels of unexpected pressure. I was in desperate need of a Barnabas or two. Regular encouragement from the pastors within my district would have given me added strength to carry on when things became unbearable. Instead, the open suspicion and verbal attacks from my colleagues pulled me in the opposite direction. The resistance I felt from my colleagues ultimately led me to question my own abilities.

Because of my own experience, I wanted to know if the support—or lack of support—made any difference in whether or not a church plant became fast-growing and dynamic. What I discovered was significant.

My survey asked each planter six questions on this topic. This series of questions used the Likert scale, from 1 to 5. An answer of 1 or 2 represented little support, 3 represented some support from a sponsoring agency, while a score of 4 or 5 represented a greater amount of support. The six questions asked were:

1. How much encouragement did you receive from your superiors?
2. How well did you feel you were supported by your pastoral colleagues?
3. How well were you accepted by surrounding churches in your denomination?
4. Did you have regular fellowship with other pastors?
5. Was your work celebrated within the denomination?
6. How much negativity did you have to overcome from your sponsoring agency?

As with conceptual freedom, this issue also used a t-test to determine significance. Any difference between the groups with a value less than .05 is considered significant. Out of the six questions asked, five significant differences were discovered in this section. The only question both groups responded equally on was the encouragement they felt from their direct superiors. In all other areas, planters leading fast-growing church plants experienced higher degrees of personal and emotional support than did those leading struggling church plants.

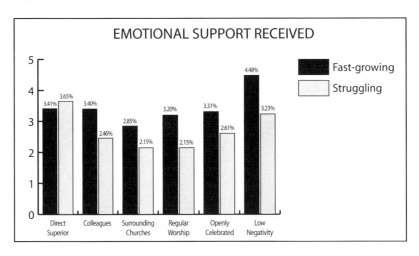

Planters leading fast-growing church plants felt significantly more support from pastoral colleagues, experienced greater acceptance from surrounding churches, had more fellowship with other pastors, were celebrated more widely in the denomination, and experienced less negativity from their sponsoring agency. Perhaps this data shows that praise only goes to the victorious. Perhaps it shows that support is often pulled out from under struggling church plants because they're floundering. Perhaps it's easier to support a church on the move. I don't, however, think this is the case, nor does it matter. If a church plant is floundering, it needs support. In any case, plants that felt more encouragement from outside sources achieved greater success. This is entirely clear.

It is vital that planters have adequate emotional support. The implications of this discovery are that the emotional health of the planter will have an effect on the emotional health of the entire fledgling congregation. If the planter is depressed and frustrated due to a lack of support and encouragement, then the church plant will suffer. Conversely, a strong sense of support from colleagues, churches, and sponsoring entities can only be beneficial for the planter as well as the plant.

My wife spoke to a group of church-planting leaders at a seminar in January 2005. She was prepared to make a few clear points about church planting, and oddly enough, I had never really seen things from her perspective until that day. Marlene walked in with a dry erase board and drew two lines, dividing the board in half. Above one of her two lines, she wrote the words "Established Church." Over the other line, she wrote, "Church Plant."

"Tell me," she said, "what kind of things happen for the pastor and his family when they come to pastor an established church? What kind of perks do they have right off the bat?"

She had these leaders hooked. Like rapid fire, they began to name the usual things.

"Security," someone answered.

"A new spiritual family," another offered.

The group continued listing perks: a paycheck, ready-made friends, a social network, and so on.

"Now," Marlene said, "what happens for the planter and his or her family when they arrive in a new city to begin their work?"

You could have heard a pin drop. Not one positive suggestion was offered, and man-oh-man was I proud of her. Like bricks falling from heaven, Marlene's point hit these men squarely over the head. It sunk in that the structures and support systems built into an already established church do not exist for the church plant.

What my wife did was simple enough, but it had an enormous impact on those church-planting leaders. Without exception, each of them confessed their need to commit to a higher quality of emotional support for those planting churches in the field. This support is critical to planting fast-growing, dynamic churches.

CHAPTER 9

Rethinking
TRAINING

WHEN I WAS IN COLLEGE, I was on the football team—or at least, they let me train with them. The first few weeks of football training were always grueling. During this time, the coach would serve up horrific portions of exercise. He had a special name for these practices: "two-a-days." I called them "Hell on earth." I was convinced that someone had forgotten to teach him how to count. We would gather every day at 6:00 a.m., and the coach would begin our routine with a two-mile run followed by a few other exercises. Then, out of the kindness of his heart, he would allow us a short break for breakfast. But we weren't done, not even close. We then headed out on the field for two hours of seemingly endless sit-ups, push-ups, squat-thrusts, and other torturous manuevers. These exercises were so intense that some of us routinely sacrificed our undigested breakfasts to the gods of football. Once we finished this battery of punishments, we were finally ready to put on the pads and do some real work. Having earned our gear, the coach spent some time making us run through a few basic play patterns. From there we went to lunch.

After lunch we got a little bit of a rest while we studied more play patterns in the classroom. Little did we know that the coach was setting us up for more. What nerve? Can you imagine? He's already drawn sweat and blood from us, and he's still not done. After studying the new plays on paper, our coach actually made us return to the field and prove that we had learned them. By the time night rolled around, it was all we could do to pull off our jerseys, take a shower, and roll into bed. As I lay in my bed, my muscles would chant in unison, "Quit, quit, quit…"

But our coach had a method and a purpose behind his cruelty. With every agonizing day of practice, he beat this into our heads and our bodies: football games are not won in the first half of the game. In fact, he liked to remind us, most are won in the final quarter. Our coach was conditioning us to be ready for the rigors and stresses of the game. We had to be ready to go the distance, and that was built through our preparation. While we never won any national championships, our team was a force to be reckoned with.

Our training for the work of Christ should be no less rigorous. After all, we are in a merciless and unceasing spiritual battle for the souls of mankind. Look at these Scriptures:

> Do you not know that in a race all the runners run, but only one receives the prize? So run that you may obtain it. Every athlete exercises self-control in all things. They do it to receive a perishable wreath, but we an imperishable. So I do not run aimlessly; I do not box as one beating the air. But I discipline my body and keep it under control, lest after preaching to others I myself should be disqualified. (1 Cor. 9:24-27 ESV)

> Study earnestly to present yourself approved to God, a workman that does not need to be ashamed, rightly dividing the Word of Truth. (2 Tim. 2:15)

> For which of you, desiring to build a tower, does not first sit down and count the cost, whether he has enough to complete it? Otherwise, when he has laid a foundation and is not able to finish, all who see it begin to mock him, saying, 'This man began to build and was not able to finish.' Or what king, going out to encounter another king in war, will not sit down first and deliberate whether he is able with ten thousand to meet him who comes against him with twenty thousand? (Luke 14:28-31 ESV)

God has not called us to be foolish about our preparation for the work he has commissioned us to do. Any denomination with plans to begin the task of planting a new church needs to focus on the issue of training. Do not misunderstand. When I mention training, I'm not speaking about seminary or any formal education. I am speaking about training that is specifically designed to prepare a church planter for work in the field.

Church planting is very different from pastoring an established church, and it requires a different set of skills. I believe these skills are a major factor in the success of fast-growing, dynamic church plants.

My sixteen years of experience behind the pulpit did not prepare me for the rigors involved in church planting. Most of what I learned about church planting I gained through reading and from a few good mentors. And strangely, these valued guides stood outside my own denomination. I was lacking a broad base of knowledge required to be an effective church planter, and though they did their best to offer some of this to me, I felt like I had been thrust onto a battlefield, straining to listen to a few good drill sergeants as they yelled life-saving advice above the sounds of gunfire. It was helpful, but it was a little too late. I would have been given a greater chance of success had I received previous and proper training.

Over the last decade, the realization that specialized training is a necessary part of good church planting has grown. Bob Logan was one of the first to offer a "boot camp" for church planters. These camps have been met with a measure of success, and this has led to the development of others. Now, dozens of parachurch organizations offer specialized training to prepare planters more adequately for the task of church planting.

In 2003, the North American Mission Board completed an analysis that studied the church-planting process of the Southern Baptist Convention. This study shows that training made a major impact on the effectiveness of their church-planting efforts. Of the churches whose pastors received this specialized training, their worship attendance was three times higher than those who received no training.[1] It is hard to deny: church-planting training is a key component in the church-planting process.

In undertaking my research, I wanted to know how training impacted the growth of a church plant. Through the survey, I asked church planters if their sponsoring agency had supplied specific church-planting training for them prior to launching their new church.

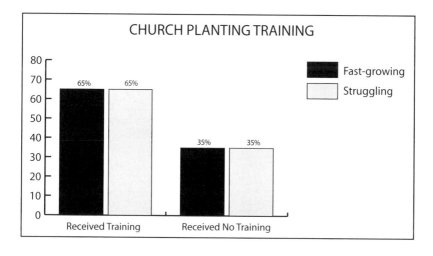

As you can see from the graph there was no significant difference between these two groups, I have to be honest, I was shocked by two pieces of data. First, I expected to see a much higher percentage of trained planters in the field. Secondly, I expected to see a significant difference between the two groups on this issue. Before getting the surveys back, I was convinced that planters leading fast-growing church plants would have received a greater degree of training than their counterparts.

The significant difference between these two groups didn't appear until the data from the next question was tallied. The planters that did receive training where asked to reveal how much training they received. This is where things got interesting.

The unfortunate planters that found themselves leading struggling church plants indicated that they, by and large, received significantly less church-planting training than did leaders of fast-growing church plants. A majority of those leading struggling church plants—a whopping 76.5 percent—received less than a week of training. Another 11.8 percent of struggling church planters received one week of training. And only 11.8 percent of those leading struggling church plants received two or more weeks of training.

By contrast, most of the leaders of fast-growing church plants received a greater amount of training. It was found that 45 percent of fast-growing church planters received more than two weeks of training. Another 28.2 percent of fast-growing church planters received at least one week of training. The final 25.6 percent of fast-growing church planters received less than a week of training.

The difference between the fast-growing and the struggling church plants, as it concerns training, is seen more dramatically if one combines the percentages behind the "at least one week's worth of training" with the "more than two weeks" groups; then, using this percent, juxtapose it against the "less than a week of training" percent. Rearranging in this way yields a very interesting result. A majority of fast-growing church plants, 74.4 percent, received one or more weeks of training. An almost equal amount of struggling church plants, 76.5 percent, received less than a week of training.

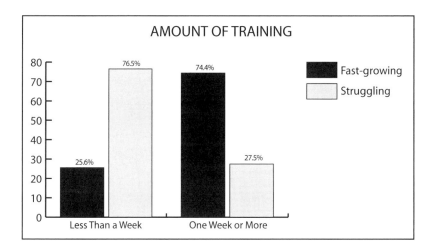

The difference between these two groups is significant. Simply put, the majority of the church planters that wound up leading fast-growing church plants received at least one week of training. The numbers make it clear: less than one week's worth of training is not enough.

The implication of this discovery is huge. Most church-planting seminars are two- to three-day events. But we have seen that two to three days of training is not enough. Whether this church-planting training is administered all at once or is broken into smaller pieces may be inconsequential. But this part of my study clearly implies that further development is needed to extend the training of our willing planters in order to better prepare them for the specialized field of church planting.

My college football coach would have never let us play against our opponents after only three days of practice. We would have embarrassed our school, our coach, and ourselves. And like my coach, most denominations would never dream of sending a missionary to a foreign field without adequate preparation. Foreign missionaries are taught extensively about the culture, traditions, and the issues pertaining to their mission field. Many missionaries spend months at language schools learning how to speak the language in order to share the gospel of Jesus Christ. Yet, when it comes to the mission field at our back door, we send church planters to a three-day seminar and wish them the best. If church planting is as important as we claim, then we must do better about training our church planters. We must train for success.

Why do I believe that training should take some extended time? A church planter needs to become proficient in multiple areas. Each planter must learn how to develop:

1. Core values

2. Vision

3. Mission statement

4. Leadership

5. Fundraising

6. Marketing strategies

7. Discipleship plans

8. Assimilation strategies

9. Budgets

10. Five to ten year goals

11. Building plans

These are only a few of the things a planter must learn. Rushing the process or short-changing it because you are trying to cram it into a three-day seminar could cause the planter to be under-prepared, and ultimately bring the church plant to a point of failure due to poor planning.

However, time isn't the only issue. The training should be of the highest quality. I did study the perceived quality each planter received. I haven't shown the information in this chapter because no significant difference was discovered between both groups of church plants. You can find this information in Appendix A. While no significant difference was discovered, as far as quality is concerned, it doesn't mean training shouldn't be done with excellence.

CHAPTER 10

No More LONE RANGERS

THE LONE RANGER is a part of American entertainment history. On Feb 2, 1933 the *Lone Ranger* episodes were launched on the radio. On Sept 14, 1949 it aired for the first time on television and ran until 1957. Throughout this run, Americans all across the nation tuned in to see their favorite masked hero take on the bad guys. Every episode ended with this lone figure yelling out a hearty, "Hi-yo Silver, away!" while his horse reared up and they rode off into the wilderness. Americans loved the Lone Ranger because he stood for truth, justice, and the American way. The Lone Ranger, riding solitary and into the sunset, became an American icon and a symbol for the rugged individualism that built this great nation.

Today, the phrase "lone ranger" is used by many preachers to denote one who may be a spiritual loner or an outcast who doesn't seem to fit neatly into the body of Christ. Ironically, most pastors fit this bill very well, and sadly, most pastors feel a lot like the Lone Ranger. These lone ranger pastors feel that they are expected, by their congregations and denominational leaders, to embody the rugged, individualistic spirit of a self-made man. They are expected to ride in, save the day, and ride off into the sunset while onlookers whisper amongst themselves, "Who was that masked man?" This expectation has caused an epidemic of health problems, burnout, infidelity, and depression among pastors in America today.

While the American pastor may suffer from this syndrome, church planters are even more susceptible. "Many church planters tend to be the rugged-individual type."[1] Their natures tend to make them willing to take on the world and their problems through their rugged, solitary will. It might even be that they prefer to take on every challenge alone; our current mode of operations surrounding church planting encourages this sort of methodology. Church planters are sent out to do work like the Lone Ranger. Most don't even get a Tonto. As leaders, I think we must ask ourselves: is sending out our church planters without any shoulder-to-shoulder or personal support even biblical?

In the sixth chapter of Mark, Jesus sent his disciples out to minister in groups of two. A quick read through the book of Acts will show that the early Church sent their missionaries out in groups of two. Come to think of it, whenever I watch the television show *COPS*, even they are sent out in groups of two. Like law enforcement, ministry is dangerous business. Don't we need to take some precautions? There is strength and safety in numbers! It's time to bring this biblical concept back into the arena of church planting. It's hard enough planting a church with support, let alone planting it solo.

Instead of one entrepreneurial planter going out to start a church on his own, why not send a team? In his book *Planting Missional Churches*, Ed Stetzer explains that a church-planting team provides "a division of gifts, and a strong leadership base."[2] Church plants that start off with a team and share the work-load stand a much better chance of reaching the 200 mark quickly.

But, does the data back that up?

Yes!

This discovery was the most significant find of the whole study. Planters were asked if they planted the church on their own or if they started with a church-planting team. A whopping 88 percent of the fast-growing church plants had a church-planting team in place prior to public launch. By contrast, only 12 percent of struggling church plants had a church-planting team. That is a difference of 76 percent between these two groups! Ouch—did I just hear the Lone Ranger take a bullet?

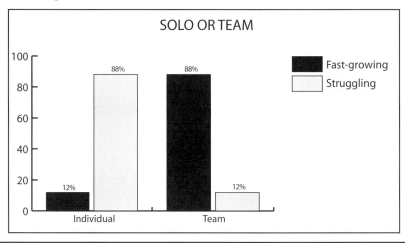

Team planting does have a positive impact on the growth of a new church, and it is a major factor that distinguishes fast-growing church plants from the comparison plants. Before the results came back to me, it was my belief that a team approach to church planting would produce a synergy unlike anything else. Because of my own experience, I already knew in my bones that those who attempted to plant a church in true Lone Ranger fashion had a much greater likelihood of struggling.

What I found even more interesting, perhaps even disturbing, was the degree of loneliness and isolation that those leading struggling church plants found themselves subjected to. Each planter was asked to indicate how many unpaid volunteer staff they had. The results were eye-opening. Not only did the majority of solo planters have no paid staff, it is significant to note that 73.1 percent of leaders involved in struggling church plants indicated that they had a grand total of zero volunteer staff. By contrast, a majority of planters leading fast-growing church plants (65 percent) had at least one volunteer to rely on.

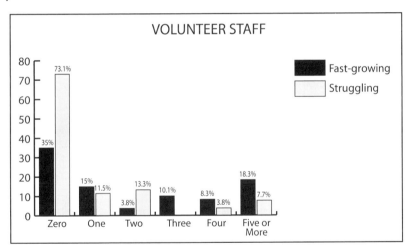

Another discovery that surfaced while researching the team planting issue was a possible optimum number of paid staff. Having too many people on the payroll can put an enormous financial strain on a new church. Of those church plants that indicated they had a planting team, I was curious to discover how many paid staff members they had aboard. According to previous data, 88 percent of fast-growing churches had a team in place prior to their public launch. While multiple paid staff were used by the fast-growing church plant group, the largest section of successful church plants (48.3 percent) only employed two people, the planter and one other staff. Looking at the chart below, it's hard to deny that this is the optimum number of paid staff members a church plant should employ prior to its public launch.

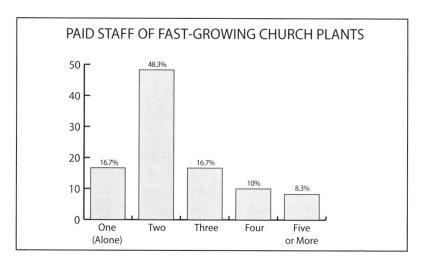

Planters leading struggling church plants can end up experiencing painful isolation. As mentioned in a previous chapter, these leaders tend to suffer significantly less support from colleagues, surrounding churches, and their sponsoring agency. To exacerbate the problem, these planters become solo planters who have little to no help at all. The vast majority of these planters are the only paid staff member and do not have any volunteer staff to rely on. Marooned on a spiritual island, they are left to build a church by their own wits and resources, to find their own avenues for healthy supporting relationships, and to shoulder the majority of the work.

By contrast, planters of fast-growing church plants usually have a team that enables them to share the workload. Teamwork makes easy work. That team also provides a built-in relational network.

I hope that this research leads us to rethink the Lone Ranger church-planting strategy. Perhaps the television Lone Ranger was able to avoid all the bullets the fictional bad guys shot his way, but this isn't a movie. It's real life. Our church planters do take spiritual bullets in this spiritual battle. Some even go down and don't get up. If you are a denominational leader, stop and ask yourself, "Is sending out a solo planter and family the wisest use of their time and energies?" The data clearly show that team planting will produce a greater likelihood of creating a strong, healthy, fast-growing church plant. It might sound funny, but every Lone Ranger deserves at least one good Tonto.

CHAPTER 11

Launch Small,
STAY SMALL

CROWDS ATTRACT CROWDS. It is a simple fact of life. John Wesley, founder of the Methodist movement, once said, "When you set yourself on fire, people love to come and see you burn." Wesley's point was that people are attracted to great happenings. In the second chapter of Acts, when the Holy Spirit descended on the disciples, what happened? "When they heard the sound, they came running to see what it was all about..." (2:6). Their response was typical of human nature. Like the people of Acts, we don't want to miss out on what's happening, so we come and watch for ourselves. The events of that day caused a buzz throughout the city of Jerusalem, and the Church was launched. That is what we attempt to do with the public launch of a new church. We are trying to create a buzz by making the first service so exciting and powerful, that people from miles around will come to see what is going on.

In 2004, I got the green light from my denomination to plant a church in central Missouri. I hit the ground running, knowing I needed to build a core group quickly. I needed to gather a group of people, in a strange city, who would help me start my new church. I was ready for the task. Months earlier, I had attended a Purpose Driven Church-planting conference. It was there I learned about a technique called "Preview Services." These types of services were specifically designed to attract a crowd, and from this crowd, I would build my core group. I was supposed to hold a preview service once a month, three to five times before the actual grand opening. These services would give me an opportunity to cast vision, build key relationships, and invite a group of people to join me on this great adventure.

In order to foster new relationships, a second technique was to be used alongside the preview service. Two weeks after each preview service, I held what the seminars called a "Comeback" event. The comeback event was designed as a more social and fun event. My first comeback event was a cookout in the park. In this casual setting, I went about gathering and building relationships while attempting to cast a clear vision of what this new church would be like. Together, these two stylized services were to be my primary avenues toward building a healthy church core group—or so I thought.

At my first preview service, I had seventy new attendees, and from this first group, I convinced four adults to join me. A month later, I had my second preview service, and there I convinced two more adults to join me. By the time the third preview rolled around, I was nervous. I had only gathered a few adults to join me. This was a result I hadn't anticipated. At the time, I was working four jobs just to make ends meet. This left me with very little time to build relationships. The third and final preview service was really disappointing. About sixty-five people attended this service, and of those only six were new families. Unfortunately, I was only able to convince three new people to join me. After the smoke cleared, these three preview services helped me gather a core group of around seventeen adults. I figured, "If twelve was good enough for Jesus, then seventeen will work for me." Sometimes, I amaze myself with such foolish optimism.

In the pit of my stomach, I knew I was in trouble. I didn't have as many adults in my core as I needed. Due to my aforementioned foolish optimism, I pushed forward in spite of my small core. In hindsight, I wish I would have slowed down and reconsidered. God had strategically placed a few good people like Ron Sylvia, Steve Sjogren, and George Hunter in my path. Each, in turn, told me to think about doing a few more preview services before marching toward an under-prepared launch. My gut wanted to listen; however, weighing in on the other side of the scales, my supervisor, my district, and my denominational colleagues all expected the launch of a new church. The pressure mounted, I made my decision, and I launched the church according to schedule. What a mistake!

On the morning of my first service, I looked out over a measly seventy-five people. It was like a punch in the stomach. I expected, and had planned for, at least two hundred. After the service, I went home depressed, frustrated, and wishing I had reconsidered. After all, I had been warned. My mentors had told me not to launch without a minimum of at least 40 adults in my core group. I wish I had listened. But the pressure I felt from my supervisor, colleagues, and peers caused me to launch despite my gut instinct. This small launch set a course for the church I could not overcome. I believe that my small launch became a self-fulfilling prophecy.

So, what does it take to launch large? How many people do I need to have in a core group prior to launching? Who should be invited to participate in the core group? How do I build my core group, and how many people will I need to launch with in order to create a buzz? Those are all good questions, and I will address them one at a time. Let's start with the core group size.

Core Group Size

A "core group" is comprised of individuals who have committed to being a part of the church plant prior to its public launch. The larger this group is, the better. In his book *Church Planting for a Greater Harvest*, Peter Wagner declares, "If the long-range plan for the church is to be under 200, the critical mass can be as small as 25 or 30 adults. However, if the plan is for the church to grow to over 200 that is too small."[1] In my opinion, core group development is one of the most crucial issues of any church plant. To launch into "public worship prior to building a significant core group is not recommend."[2] If a new church is to grow rapidly and gain significant momentum, the planter must build a large core group.

In 2000, Dennis Powell conducted a study that revealed that church plants which start without a core group are more likely to fail. Of the twenty-five church plants he studied, five had no core group prior to launching, and all five of these church plants closed within five years.[3] A church plant must generate a crowd quickly if it is to survive. If the church planter is not able to build a large enough core, the planter and core group will never be able to pull off the kind of launch needed to generate a buzz. Remember, crowds attract crowds.

If this initial core group is too small, a close-knit, family atmosphere may set in. I believe that I experienced this problem in my church. Those who attended the public service subconsciously assumed that this church was going to be a small, intimate church. One family that attended the first Sunday called up their relatives and invited them to come and visit their new church. Soon this family was the largest group in the church, and they settled in for a long ride. It wasn't long before the initial excitement fizzled, and people stopped inviting their neighbors. I've always imagined that they must have nudged one another among the pews and whispered quietly, "This is such a nice and small family church, and that is just what we were looking for." That is not to say that there is anything wrong with a small, intimate church, but that was not what I was trying to create. A small core group tends to limit the word-of-mouth excitement that is so necessary to the growth of the church.

How many do you need in a core group prior to launch? In the survey, I asked planters to indicate how many adults they had in their core group prior to the public launch of the church. Two major differences were discovered from this question. A majority of struggling church plants, 69.2 percent, had twenty-five individuals or less in their core group prior to public launch. The second largest group of struggling church plants, 19 percent, had a starting core group of between twenty-six and fifty people before launching. Consequently, after three years, most of these church plants, still remained small.

By contrast, only 20 percent of fast-growing church plants had less than twenty-five people in their core group. The largest grouping among the fast-growing church plants, 55 percent, had a core group of twenty-six to fifty people. Do you see a pattern emerging? The fast-growing church plants, by a large majority, had more individuals involved in the core group prior to launch than did struggling plants. Among fast-growing church plants, the healthy minimum of individuals involved in the core group was twenty-six to fifty. Only one-fifth of fast-growing church plants reported having less.

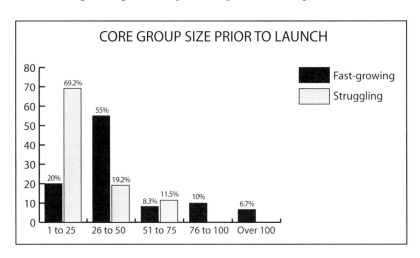

(Note: Many of the planters involved in this study did me a big favor by writing the actual number of individuals in their core group beside the question. The actual average was about forty.)

In essence, starting small leads to thinking small, and this becomes a self-fulfilling prophecy. Gaining a critical mass is incredibly vital to rapid growth. Groups attract groups. This is not a myth; this is a group dynamic fact. If a church plant wishes to launch big, it will need plenty of workers: ushers, greeters, nursery volunteers, teen and children leaders, musicians, and a large group to help set up and tear down equipment. A small core group equals few ministries offered to the attendees of the public launch. (Let me briefly mention, fast-growing church plants generally had at least three basic ministries in place for their public launch: adult worship, children's services, and teen ministries. I will share more on this later.) A church plant that starts with a small core group that has to shoulder all of the extra work will tire if other workers are not raised up quickly.

According to the data gathered, nearly 70 percent of struggling church plants had twenty-five or fewer people involved in their core group prior to launch. By contrast, 80 percent of fast-growing church plants had twenty-six or more people in the core group. Repeat after me, "Large core, good. Small core, bad." This discovery shows that in order for a church plant to launch large, it should have more than twenty-six adults involved in the core group prior to the day the church goes public.

Gathering A Core

Fast-growing church plants reported a significantly higher number of adults in their core group than struggling church plants. So what was the best way to gather a larger core group? I looked at the two most popular methods of building a core group: small groups and preview services.

Let's start with the struggling church plant group. The largest number of the leaders of struggling church plants, 46.2 percent, used small groups as the primary avenue for building a core group. Another 16.9 percent of struggling church plants relied heavily on the preview services as a means for building the core group. Therefore we see that 63 percent of the struggling church plants were one-dimensional in their approach to building a core group.

Now let's take a look at the fast-growing church plants. Of this group, 55 percent tended to be multi-dimensional in attracting a following of people. These planters used a more healthy combination of small groups and preview services to build their core group.

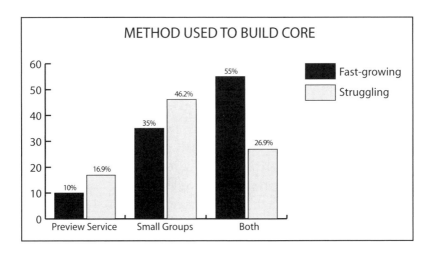

What surprised me most about this finding was the low percentage—
only 10 percent—of fast-growing churches using the preview services as the
primary method of building a core group. I was just as surprised to note that
many more fast-growing church plants relied on small groups over preview
services. From this, I am able to make the minor conclusion that the relationships being built within these small groups are more beneficial than the glitz
and glamor of a well-planned preview service.

It would appear from the data that a two-pronged approach, an approach
that utilizes a healthy dose of both small groups and preview services, is the
best way to go about building a large core group. Relying too heavily on one
method is most likely a mistake.

"Seed" Family Involvement

So, who should make up a church plant's core group? This might sound
like an odd question, but there are varying philosophies on this topic. Some
believe that the church planter should only utilize new converts because
churched people, with their preconceived notions of the church experience,
can be difficult to deal with. Others believe that the planter needs a small base
of churched people to help build a core since they, at least, have some idea of
what a church should do. Who is right?

My survey asked each planter to share what percentage of their core group
was made up of "seed" families from other churches. A seed family is a family
who intentionally joins the new church plant from a mother church. A seed
family is a group that is already experienced in Christian tradition. They have
not made this move because they are disgruntled with their former church.
They are a Christian family or unit who knew about, planned for, and inten-

tionally and strategically became a part of the church plant with the blessing of their pastor. By default, all other individuals who become a part of the church plant's core group are not considered a seed family.

Let's start with the struggling church plants. A majority of struggling church plants, 62 percent, had no seed families involved in their core group. That means that these struggling plants had either no core group, or else their group was made up of new converts, seekers, church hoppers, or individuals who joined the core once the planter made a plea for followers. Only 38 percent of struggling church plants had seed families in their core group. By contrast, 35 percent of fast-growing church plants indicated that they had no seed families. The remaining 65 percent had seed families involved in their core group.

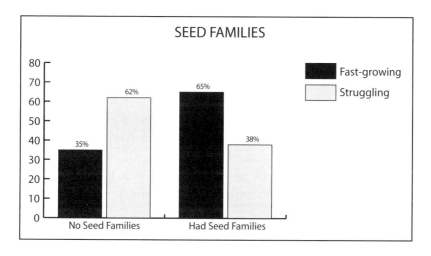

This is a significant finding. Why? These seed families bought into the vision of the church and carried a portion of the load for this new church. They were more than likely tithing, working, and taking on ministries from the beginning. Because of their experience, they knew what they were committing to. Starting a church without any seed families in the core group is a risky and punishing strategy. If a planter waits until he or she is on the field before gathering a core, he or she might end up being stuck with a group of spiritually immature, or even pre-Christian, people. Don't get me wrong; these are the people we are trying to reach. But if the needs of a young church grind the new convert into the ground with unexpected responsibilities, trouble will quickly arise.

Chances are, a spiritually immature or pre-Christian person simply won't understand what you are attempting to do. They won't have the sense of ownership and may not be willing to sacrifice in the way the planter needs them to. Likewise, new converts tend to have little idea of what it takes to "do" church. The bottom line is, a church planter needs to have a handful of sold-out believers who understand Jesus and the church.

I believe my findings reveal that, in many cases, a loving mother church was involved. These mother churches must have had vision enough to send out a large contingent of its families to start another church. Whatever the case, this study reveals that it is far healthier to have "seed" families involved in the core group. Even though a church plant is targeting the lost, it needs a base of mature believers willing to make the sacrifices that it takes to propel a young church into the future. I'm not saying that it can't be done without them, but I am saying that these more mature core group members will keep a few hiccups out of the growth process.

Number of Preview Services

Even though one of the findings above showed that preview services should not be relied on as the primary method for building a core group, nonetheless, they do help introduce the church plant to the community. A preview is a church service held once a month for the purpose of helping potential Christians and new members understand what the future church will look like. Both groups of church plants, 65 percent of the fast-growing and 53.8 percent of the struggling church plants, used preview services in one form or fashion. So, if a church planter chooses to use preview services, how many should he hold before the public launch of the church? Is there a magic number?

According to the Purpose Driven Model, anyone using preview services should hold at least three but no more than five. Part of the genius of this method is the use of a "comeback" service, a casual and fun event held two weeks after the preview service. This event is to be used by the planter to build relationships and cast a clear and more personable vision to interested individuals. It was strongly recommended to me that I hold no more than five preview services. In my case this formula didn't lead to a successful launch. That's not to say that this was the reason for my poor numbers; it was just one piece of the pie. I now have research that examines the numbers of preview services utilized by other church plants.

This part of the survey yielded eye-opening results: fast-growing church plants held far more preview services than struggling church plants. Almost 70 percent of struggling church plants held three or fewer preview services prior to public launch. On the other hand, a stunning 94 percent of fast-growing church plants held three or more preview services. In fact, almost half of the fast-growing church plants, 46 percent, held five or more preview services.

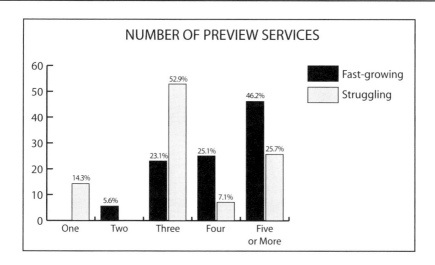

Interestingly enough, of the fast-growing church plants that held five or more preview services, many of them indicated that they held these services two times a month. This means that they hit the community hard by holding a preview service every other week. Also the comeback service was not used as often in these cases. What are we to make of this finding? My belief is that a heightened frequency of events and attendee contact is needed to build momentum. According to the data, the build-up to the launch is best if it is fast and frequent. When a church plant is trying to gather totally unchurched or dechurched individuals, people who are not used to coming to church, a monthlong build-up may be too long. The seekers being targeted may not be ready to attend on a weekly basis, and a month may be too long, which leaves a narrow window of opportunity.

Launch Day Size

If a newcomer looks around on that first day and sees a lot of excited people, he or she will feel even more excited and proud of the new church. In turn, they will be more likely to come again the next Sunday and invite their friends. If enough of these newcomers get excited and create a buzz in the community, this will lead to a higher probability of breaking through the all-important 200 barrier.

The size of the crowd at the public launch usually sets the pace for the development of the new church. Schaller explains this point by writing, "Starting small often creates a form of a self-fulfilling cycle of performance while starting large usually sends the new mission down the road to a radically different approach to ministry."[4] That first day sets the stage for the all-important critical mass. So, what was the launch day size of fast-growing church plants?

The survey data revealed three significant differences concerning the size of the first public service. Of the struggling church plants, 65 percent had fifty or fewer people attend their first public service. Of the fast-growing church plants, only 10 percent had fifty or fewer attendees come to the public launch of the church. For both the fast-growing and struggling church plants, around 15 percent attracted a crowd of fifty-one to one hundred attendees for their first public service. These are very telling numbers, especially when we observe the remaining portion of the data. Note that the vast majority of fast-growing church plants, an astounding 75 percent of them, attracted one hundred or more individuals on their first Sunday. Only 19.2 percent of struggling church plants were able to accomplish this feat.

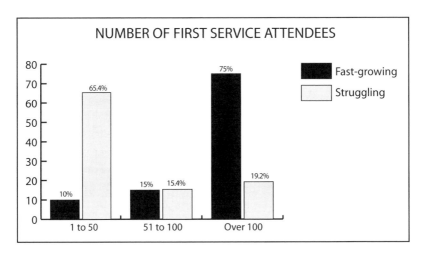

As before, combining the data gives a clearer view of the significant attendance differences between fast-growing and struggling church plants. A huge amount of struggling church plants, 80.8 percent, launched with fewer than 100 attendees at their first service. By contrast, 75 percent of the fast-growing church plants had over one hundred attendees present at their first service. The evidence here is about as clear as it gets. Looking at these two hard statistics, it seems to me that planters should strive for a minimum of one hundred attendees for that first service.

If a launch occurs with anything smaller, stop, and rethink your strategy. It might even be wise to return to the preview services and launch at another time. Remember, most of these struggling church plants that launched small, stayed small.

I'll say it again: crowds attract crowds. To create new missions that break out of the mold of the self-serving, survival-minded, family-run organizations, leaders must find a way to plant churches that grow rapidly in size in a very short period of time. When a church is able to grow rapidly and gain momentum, it will foster a healthy, outreach-minded attitude among the members.

Church plants that do not quickly grow beyond the 200 average in attendance within a few years will lose momentum and fall into the small-church trap. This stagnation of growth will result in a lowered sense of congregational self-esteem. Church plants are more vulnerable to low morale due to heightened expectations for success. When not met with immediate success, most church plants fall prey to discouragement.

Once an attitude of defeat settles into the hearts and minds of the church planter and the new congregation, they begin to view themselves "as small, weak, unattractive, powerless and frustrated with a limited future."[5] Unfortunately, this attitude is the state in which many church plants find themselves.

Now that you've waded through the charts, graphs, and puzzling statistics, let me summarize the findings revealed in this chapter.

- Any church plant seeking to reach a fast-growing level will need somewhere between twenty-six and fifty adults in a core group prior to launch.

- A multi-dimensional approach utilizing both small groups and preview services should be used to build this core group.

- If a church planter chooses to use preview services, he or she should consider holding more than three—possibly one every other week for a few months.

- The core group should be made up of a handful of committed, intentionally placed seed families who own the vision of the church.

- Finally, the planter should plan for and expect over one hundred attendees on the first Sunday.

CHAPTER 12

Planning for GROWTH

THE FINAL PART OF THE RESEARCH covered the various strategies employed by church plants. Every church, whether new or established, needs a good strategy. One problem I've found with church-planting books is that every author has his or her own opinion about what works and what doesn't. These varying opinions do not help when there is such a broad range of strategic decisions that every planter must make before launching a new church: What kind of ministries should be in place at the time of going public? What kind of music should be used during worship services? What kind of facility should be used? All of these questions and many more need to be answered prior to launch. There is no doubt that a good strategy is vital to the development of any church.

The questions contained in the survey focused on four strategic issues every church planter must wrestle with: types of ministries in place, style of worship, facility, and stewardship. I sought to discover whether there was an optimum strategy in the planting of fast-growing church plants.

Ministries in Place

Having multiple ministries in place at the time of the first public worship is a must. Anyone wishing to plant a church in this era of abundant choices and options must be prepared to offer the unchurched multiple points of connection. Some experts studying the church-planting arena believe that building a multi-dimensional ministry should be a slow process. A new church should be "willing to move along at a slow pace."[1] Still, others teach all ministries must be in place at the time of public launch. These ministries can include everything from children's ministries to senior adult ministries. In the survey, I decided to ask the planters what kinds of ministries they had in place at the time of public launch. With this information, I would be able to see if the amount or types of ministries offered at the time of launch caused any difference between fast-growing and struggling church plants. What I discovered was significant. How these two groups approached the issue of available ministries is nothing short of incredible.

Fast-growing and struggling church plants had a radically different use of both children and teen ministries. Of the fast-growing church plants, a total of 96.7 percent had a children's ministry and 48.3 percent had a teen ministry in place at the time of public launch. Of the struggling church plants, only 42.3 percent had a children's ministry and 15.4 percent had a teen ministry in place at the time of public launch. That's a staggering 54.4 percent difference between the fast-growing and the struggling churches that employed a children's ministry during their public launch, and a 32.9 percent difference between the fast-growing and the struggling churches that offered a teen ministry right away. What makes one sit up and take notice is that the majority of struggling church plants offered nothing more than a worship service to attendees at the time of public launch. Simply put, fast-growing churches offered more ministry choices from the beginning.

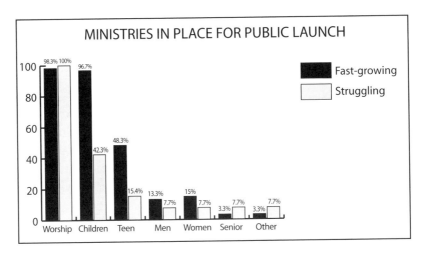

Let me repeat, fast-growing church plants were offering multiple connection points from the start. One significant difference that doesn't jump right out of this chart is the total number of ministries both groups had in place at the time of public launch. The next chart shows that almost 92 percent of fast-growing church plants offered three or more ministry opportunities at their opening. On the other hand, 64 percent of the struggling church plants offered only an adult worship service to first-time attendees.

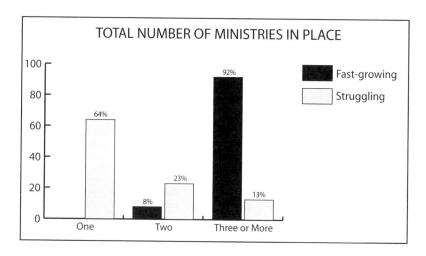

According to the previous chart, the majority of the fast-growing churches had three ministries in place for their launch: Worship, Children, and Teen. We can call this the "Holy Trinity" of ministries. This combination seems to separate the struggling from the fast-growing church plants. In any case, the data show that whatever ministries are made available, multiple points of contact are far more beneficial than a one-dimensional approach.

Rick Warren said, "When I started Saddleback Church, all we offered for the first year was a worship service and a limited children's church program. We didn't attempt to be a full service church."[2] Although he tells others not to do what he did, it's hard to argue with his success and the authority it has given him. But while this approach may have worked twenty years ago, we live in a different world from when Saddleback was started. I believe Rick's statement, and others like his, has unintentionally helped perpetuate the idea that all a church plant needs to offer for the first year is an adult worship service.

My data actually shows the very opposite. Churches that began without a full service agenda struggled, while churches that offered services for various age groups became fast-growing churches. In a culture where Americans are constantly offered multiple choices, it only makes sense to offer as many contact points as possible. Logic dictates that many parents are bringing their children to church to help instill in them some form of moral education. The church that is able to offer a quality service to these young families and their children will have a greater potential to retain them. As a parent, my sentiment is that I love to go to church, but my children need to be taught as well. If I had to choose between two churches, I would choose the one that offers a program for my children.

Style of Worship

In a study performed by Dr. Ed Stetzer in conjunction with the North American Mission Board (NAMB) of the Southern Baptist Convention, they discovered that the style of worship used by their new churches had a significant impact on the attendance after a four-year period. This study revealed that the worship styles that correspond with large attendance numbers were contemporary, seeker-sensitive, and blended.[3] Over the last decade, conventional wisdom and a modernization of the American church service has promoted these forms of worship as the most effective, and now Dr. Stetzer's research has given credible evidence that these styles are consistently producing larger crowds. My research intended to examine these worship styles in a broader context. Here is what I discovered.

According to the survey, an overwhelming majority, 75 percent, of the fast-growing church plants used a contemporary style of worship. By contrast, far fewer struggling church plants, 42.3 percent of them, used a contemporary worship style. Another 34.6 percent of the struggling church plants made use of a blended style of worship, and 19.2 percent used a more traditional style of worship.

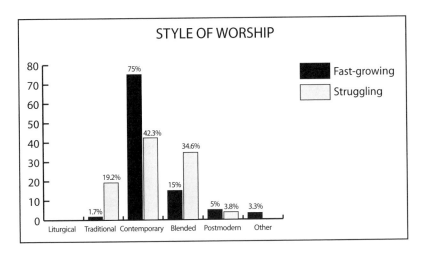

Paul tells us to become all things to all men, in order that we might win some. I think this finding speaks to this issue. Stop and think about it for a minute. Who are you trying to reach? What kind of music do they listen to? What TV programs do they watch? Where do they hang out? You must be able to effectively exegete your culture and community if you are going to have an impact.

If you are targeting an older group, by all means, start a church using a traditional model. I believe there may be a time and a place for starting a traditional church. However, only 2 percent of fast-growing church plants used a traditional style of worship. Be sensitive to your surroundings, even if it means using a style that is outside your comfort zone.

A church plant should be started in a way that is contextually relevant to the culture surrounding it. We are to be incarnate in the culture of which Jesus called us to be a part. Remember, Jesus came to a specific culture at a specific time in history. He came to the Jews, not the Gentiles. He took part in the rituals, traditions, and rules of the culture he came to. He didn't come as a Roman, Greek, Phoenician, or Mead. He came as a Jew! So, if the planter comes to a large city, he must know what it is to be cosmopolitan. And if the planter plants among country folk, he'd better have their specific church preferences in mind.

Facility

Where should we worship? There are many kinds of buildings a church plant can start in, and the type of facility used by a church plant is somewhat important. Schaller explains that the type of facility used to host the church plant will affect the perception people have of the new church. The risk involved in choosing the wrong facility "is that potential future members may drift away when they realize the limitations on programming" due to the facility chosen to house the church plant.[4] My research, however, did not reveal this issue to be an incredibly significant factor. The survey asked planters what type of facility they started in, and the resulting data revealed very little difference between the fast-growing and the struggling church plants.

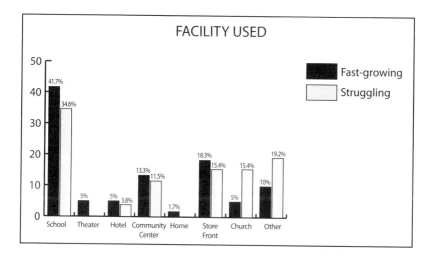

I have included this graph, not because of any major differences, but rather as a point of interest to show the various types of facilities that are being used. Notice that the type of facility used most often by both groups was a school. The only noticeable percentage difference between the two groups was discovered in the use of church buildings. But, the difference is not great enough to qualify as significant.

Financial Stewardship

The final area studied among these church plants was the issue of stewardship. A lot of debates rage in churches and among church leaders about when it is proper to introduce the concept of financial stewardship to the new believer. In many church-planting training seminars, I have heard that the planter should not talk about money within the first year of the church's existence. At the same time, several leading researchers in the arena of church planting argue that the early introduction of stewardship is a critical factor affecting the size and survivability of a new church.

In fact, one researcher showed a consistent and marked difference between those new churches that expected members to tithe from those that did not. According to this research, after four years, church plants that expected tithing experienced an average attendance of 120. Those new churches that did not teach any form of financial stewardship averaged around ninety in attendance.[5] I wanted to know how stewardship teaching affected the growth and ultimate self-support of a church plant.

In order to study these issues, my survey asked the church planters if they taught financial stewardship to their new congregations within the first six months of the public launch. I discovered that the teaching of financial stewardship was a factor in a church plant becoming fast growing.

A total of 56.7 percent of fast-growing church planters indicated that they taught stewardship within the first six months, while 38.5 percent of planters leading struggling church plants, indicated that they taught on stewardship within that time period. These results show a significant difference of 18.2 percent. Remember, anything above 15 percent difference is considered significant.

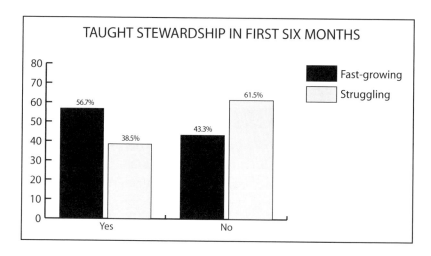

Dr. Dennis Powell takes this issue a step further. In his research on church plant survival rates, the new churches that gave at least 3 percent of their total income to outreach and missions reached self-support more quickly than those churches that did not.[6] This shows that corporate tithing is a crucial step that helps new churches reach self-support quickly.

I've heard both sides of the argument. Some say that seekers should not be pushed to give because they believe the church is all about money in the first place. Others say that even seekers understand that it costs to "do" church. My data shows that a significantly higher percentage of fast-growing church plants taught on financial stewardship within the first six months. I'm sure this was a major factor in their transition to self-support, but I also believe it helped their growth. Quickly teaching attendees about the need to give will naturally accelerate a church's ability to do ministry. Think about it; if a church has more finances, it is able to meet more needs. If it meets more needs, it will attract more people.

Giving to Missions

It is important for a new church to implant an outward focus within the DNA of the church. The spirit of the Great Commission does not come to its journey's end at the doors of the church plant. However, many plants overly concerned about their own survival will naturally reduce their focus on outreach and missions. While most burgeoning churches claim to be concerned with outreach and evangelism, their actual budget for such ministries tells more about priorities than any amount of lip service.

I was curious to see if fast-growing and struggling church plants differed greatly in corporate tithing; I asked how much each plant allocated for missions and outreach each month from their general funds. The data returned in the survey revealed that a significantly higher number of fast-growing church plants, 80 percent of them, gave 10 percent or more toward outreach and missions. Of the struggling church plants, only 41.3 percent gave at this level. This shows a 38.7 percent difference between the two groups. Only 3.3 percent of fast-growing church plants gave a dismal 4 percent or less toward missions and outreach. And due to what I can only assume to be the survivalist mentality setting in, 43.3 percent of the struggling church plants gave 4 percent or less to missions and outreach. In this 0 to 4 percent range, we are left with a 40 percent difference between the struggling and the fast-growing church plants.

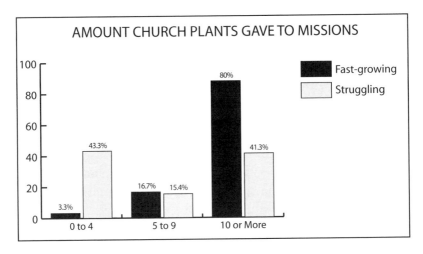

An inward-focused church plant tends to have a higher probability of remaining a struggling church plant. The Scriptures continually remind us that God blesses obedience. Malachi 3:10 says, "'Bring the whole tithe into the storehouse, that there may be food in my house. Test me in this,' says the Lord Almighty, 'and see if I will not throw open the floodgates of heaven and pour out so much blessing that you will not have room enough for it.'" According to God's Word, tithing from the blessing God has given us has never been an option, but an expectation. Since the act of planting a new church is a spiritual endeavor, it cannot be discounted that a plant's commitment, or lack of commitment, to tithe has a direct effect on the church.

The idea that a church plant should be required to tithe may seem counterintuitive, yet it is biblically sound. New churches need all the money they can find in the early days, but we know the Bible tells us that God blesses our faithfulness. Some may ask churches to begin small and work their way up to a tithe. My reply to that is this: does Jesus ask us to obey in pieces and work our way up, or does he ask for complete and immediate obedience from us?

I could go into a twenty-minute sermon about obedience and our responsibility to tithe, but I won't. I could rant wildly about how pastors ask their members to tithe and how hypocritical it is for a church not to do what it asks its members to do, but I won't. I could foam at the mouth while mentioning all the Scriptures that explicitly state what Jesus thought of sharing and giving, but I won't. I will, however, mention that our church plants can never expect to receive God's blessing if they are not obeying His word.

CHAPTER 13

Where Do We Go FROM HERE?

IN THE FIRST CHAPTER I shared my personal and disappointing church-planting experience. This painful experience resulted in my being plagued by feelings of failure, incompetence, and frustration. I couldn't understand why the church I planted had not grown at the pace others had. In many ways, the findings of this study have helped me understand at least a few of the reasons behind my own frustrating church-planting experience.

Before starting my endeavor, I had been confident that I was designed to do the work of a planter. My personality profile fit the bill perfectly and I scored very high on the Ridley assessment. I simply *knew* in my gut that I was headed for a wild ride and would soon be pastoring the next great mega church.

But in actuality, I was lacking. Even though I am an avid reader and learned all I could about church planting on my own, I was given little training designed to help me understand what I was about to do. Furthermore, the support systems my wife and I counted on from our district weren't there. Instead we experienced anger, suspicion, and jealousy. After some time in the field, my wife and I began to feel a great sense of isolation and negativity from the group we served. This probably had something to do with the four different jobs I had to work (beyond the ministry) in order to make ends meet for my family. This pace, as well as the pressures of dealing with our own sponsors, left us both exhausted and frustrated. All the while, discouragement was creeping in because of the church plant's slow progress.

Eventually, I received some additional funding from my sponsoring agency, but it was too little, too late. The church had launched and my window to create an atmosphere of excellence had passed. Through all my attempts, I was only able to secure seventeen adults in my core group prior to launch. I didn't realize it at the time, but I wasn't ready to go public. On the day of the big launch, a total of sixty-five individuals, adults as well as children, showed up at the grand opening. In spite of my best efforts, we never broke out of that small-church mold.

Further, finances became a huge problem because I decided not to teach on any form of financial stewardship; I didn't want to scare away those I was trying to reach. As a result, offerings were severely hampered and we could barely pay the bills. The church budget wouldn't even allow for any giving beyond our own survival.

Okay, okay, I'm done. I'm done rolling around in the factors that left painful impressions on my psyche. I will one day release all of this experience into the hands of the Father, but for now, I sting like any other human. What I *can* do for now is realize that I have a much better understanding of the factors that contributed to the stunted growth of my church plant.

In May 2006 I began to put this new information into practice, to put my research to the test. After all, none of this means much if it is nothing more than a simple collection of facts and figures. The question yet to be answered was: does it work?

The first church plant modeled after this research would be located in Wesley Chapel, FL. Everything was set in place for a huge launch. We held our breath and prayed for the best. On September 10th, 2006 we opened with 324 first-time visitors. Today, one year later, the church is running 280 in attendance, has experienced sixty-five conversions, and, if all goes well, is set to soar well beyond the 500 mark within the next one- and one-half years.

Before I close out this book, I'd like to acknowledge that not every planter, denomination, or sponsoring agency is interested in planting a large church. I do understand and recognize that large churches are not the only valid ministries in the United States. In the right environment, a small church can be just as effective as a large church. It would be ridiculous of me to believe that the Holy Spirit only inhabits large churches.

After planting four churches, assisting with the planting of four more, and now leading a church-planting movement, I am confident that I am on to something. Millions of dollars are spent each year attempting to plant churches around the United States and most of these attempts garner only meager results. I believe that we can no longer be satisfied with substandard attempts. If church planting, as Peter Wagner states, is the greatest form of evangelism under heaven, then we must give it perfect attention. Future attempts at church planting must be pursued with knowledge and excellence.

We must discover new and innovative ways to reach out to an American population that is dying spiritually.

For those of you who have read this book and appreciate the discoveries made, here is a bird's eye view of what I believe it takes to plant a fast-growing, dynamic church. As I have mentioned before, it is important to understand that each of these findings existed in varying degrees in both fast-growing and struggling church plants. So, it isn't wise to put too much importance on any one finding. Instead, the significance of this study must be viewed holistically.

The results of this study revealed that significant differences did exist between fast-growing and struggling church plants.

1. Using the Ridley assessment is a must. No planter should be allowed on the field unless he or she has been properly assessed. When looking for a planter that can break out and overcome the 200 barrier, look for an above average planter. Those who led fast-growing, dynamic church plants had an average score of 4.26, while those leading struggling church plants scored an average of 3.82.

2. Adequate financial support of a church plant is a must. Church planting is expensive and requires a proper balance of funding from the sponsoring agency. The financing of this plant should come through a combination of sponsoring agency and planter. Every planter should take ownership and be personally involved in raising extra funds. If you find a planter who is not willing or able to do this, he or she may be the wrong person. Keep in mind that funding these new churches requires a lot of thought, because a delicate balance exists between giving a planter too much or too little financial support.

3. A majority of fast-growing church plants were led by full-time planters. Don't let your planter go out and struggle to survive. Give planters the ability to focus fully on the task at hand. If he or she becomes overly worried about earning a living, this extra concern splits the planter's attention, causing a diminished ability to maintain an intense focus on the church plant.

4. A majority of full-time planters leading fast-growing church plants received salary support for two years or less. Nearly 80 percent of the planters involved in struggling church plants received salary support for three to five years. This data seems to imply that an extended period of support is not good for a new church. It may be that the security offered by this extension causes a window of procrastination that is detrimental to the development of the church plant.

5. A higher percentage of the planters involved in fast-growing, dynamic church plants received additional financial support past the initial salary given. While I did not ask about the specifics of this additional support, I believe that this extra funding was given as a start-up grant for the church. More than likely it was used to purchase equipment or to do advertising.

6. While a higher percentage of fast-growing, dynamic church plants received additional funding, most received $50,000 or less within a one-year time frame. A significant number of struggling church plants received over $50,000 in a four- or five-year period. Again, too much money given to a new start may be just as detrimental as too little.

7. Planters of fast-growing, dynamic church plants were far more involved in raising additional financial support beyond what their sponsoring agency gave them. A sponsoring agency should develop a program to assist the planter in raising awareness of funding needs.

8. The vision for a church plant must be birthed in the heart of the individual planting the church. Earlier, I told a story about a denominational leader who asked a pastor to start a church in a place that he had never considered. As a result, the planter tried, but the vision cast by the leader withered. While this may not be the case in every instance, the data reveals a greater likelihood for a church plant to become a fast-growing plant if the vision comes from the individual planting the church.

9. Freedom to choose the target audience was also another significant factor. The leaders of fast-growing church plants had far more freedom to choose the type of audience they wanted to target for the plant.

10. Planters of fast-growing, dynamic church plants were given more freedom to spend their funding in the ways they saw fit.

11. Overall, less control and/or management from the sponsoring agency was exerted over fast-growing, dynamic church plants. The data indicated that sponsoring agencies need to give proper freedoms to the church planter instead of imposing a cookie-cutter church-planting plan. Those church plants that were a part of the struggling group tended to have more constraints and control placed over them.

12. It is vital that planters have adequate emotional support. Strong and immediate human networks should be set up for the transplanted church planter. The emotional health of the planter, be it good or bad, will have an effect on the emotional health of the entire fledg-

ling congregation. Planters of fast-growing, dynamic church plants felt significantly more support from pastoral colleagues, experienced acceptance from surrounding churches, had more fellowship with other pastors, were celebrated more widely in their denomination, and experienced less negativity from their sponsoring agency.

13. Sponsoring agencies must develop a quality training program. Leaders of fast-growing, dynamic church plants received one or more weeks of training designed to prepare them for church planting. By contrast, planters involved in struggling church plants indicated that they had received less than one week of training.

14. Planting a church with a team of at least two paid staff is a must! Please don't send a planter and family out to plant a church as a lone ranger. An overwhelming majority of the leaders of fast-growing, dynamic church plants, 88.3 percent, indicated that they started with a team. On the other side of the scales, 88.5 percent of church planters leading struggling church plants indicated that they started the church on their own. Don't underestimate the strength found in numbers.

15. Fast-growing church plants reported a significantly higher number of adults in their core group prior to launch. Any church plant that doesn't have at least 40 people in their core group prior to launch should reconsider launching.

16. According to the survey results, fast-growing church plants had at least three basic ministries in place at the time of public launch: adult worship, children's services, and teen ministries. We live in a very unforgiving culture. Parents may be willing to try a church once or twice, but if you can't provide something exciting and meaningful for their children, you will lose their interest quickly.

17. Fast-growing church plants not only used preview services but also utilized small groups to build their core group. Don't be one-dimensional about building your core group.

18. Leading up to the public launch, leaders of fast-growing church plants used five or more preview services on a bi-weekly basis. Unchurched and dechurched people have so much on their plates every week that you are likely to get squeezed out. Consider having "practice" services once every other week. Waiting for a whole month to do another preview is far too long. Frequent connections are key.

19. Fast-growing church plants launched with a larger number of attendees at the first public service. Do everything within your power to get

"butts in the seats." Thank the Lord for every warm body you can get. You have to create a buzz in the community if you are going to gain momentum.

20. Among the fast-growing church plants, most were taught about the importance of finances within the first six months. Don't think for a moment that unchurched people don't know it takes money to run a church. Don't be shy about letting people know. Don't be overbearing, don't whine, and don't be secretive about your finances. The way to fight the preconceived notions of the unchurched about money scandals in the church is with openness. Be transparent about what you do with the money and people will be more likely to give.

21. Lastly, fight like mad to keep your ministry focused outward. If you don't do it at the beginning, it will be hard to institute later on. A high percentage of fast-growing church plants tithed from the beginning, while struggling church plants tended to be inward-focused with their money. Over 40 percent of them gave less than 4 percent of their income to missions and outreach.

I understand that many other factors go into the planting of a church. The factors listed in the book were not intended to be an exhaustive list. They do, however, provide a good overview of some significant differences between fast-growing and struggling church plants. While not a guarantee for success, I am fully convinced that those who implement these findings will have a greater likelihood of starting a fast-growing, dynamic church plant. May God bless you as you join him in the great adventure of planting a new church.

Other
FINDINGS

THE FOLLOWING TOPICS WERE STUDIED, but no significant differences were discovered between fast-growing and struggling church plants. Please understand that these findings and/or issues are important to church planting, but within the constraints of this study, there were not statistically significant differences.

Remember that a significant difference was discovered when fast-growing and struggling church plants were separated by a 15 percent difference on any given question. The findings below, while interesting and beneficial, did not qualify as significant.

These findings are valuable for setting guidelines and forming church-planting systems that can lead to healthier church plants.

Salary Support

Salary support of any pastor is a critical issue. Planters were asked about the kind of salary support they received from their sponsoring agency. The possible choices were: full salary, partial salary, or no salary. Of the fast-growing church plants, 26.6 percent reported receiving a full salary, 48.3 percent received a partial salary, and 25 percent received no salary benefit from their sponsoring agency. Struggling church plants reported similar percentages: 30.7 percent received a full salary, 38 percent received a partial salary, and 30.7 percent received no salary.

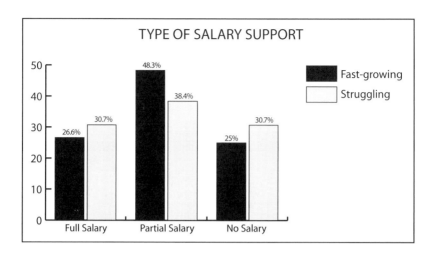

While both fast-growing and struggling church planters were similar, I found it interesting to discover the most frequently used form of salary for both groups was a partial salary. I had expected this to be a significant difference. Prior to this study I believed that pastors leading fast-growing church plants would have received a full salary at a much higher percentage than struggling church plants. While there was no significant difference, this finding does have value for those leading church-planting movements, as it concerns setting guidelines for salary structures.

Help with the Purchase of Property

Only 10 percent of both fast-growing and struggling church plants indicated they had received any help from a sponsoring agency with the purchase of property. I have heard some church planters remark, "If only my denomination would help me purchase some property, we could build a church and fill it." Many have treated the purchasing of property and the erecting of a structure like the planting of magic beans. Understand that this finding does not reveal whether a church plant purchased property or erected a building it only shows if a sponsoring agency helped purchase property.

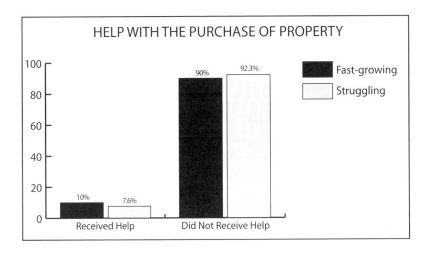

Temporary Structure

I will say from personal experience that a church plant which remains in a temporary structure for more than two years runs the risk of losing momentum. Constantly tearing down and setting up takes its toll on leadership and gives the attendees a sense of homelessness. My personal opinion is that a church plant should plan to be in a building of its own by the end of the third year.

Percentage of Help with Property

Of the fast-growing church plants that received help purchasing property, 66 percent received up to 50 percent financial help or less, and 34 percent received over 51 percent financial help. Of the struggling church plants that received help with the purchase of property, 50 percent received up to 50 percent financial help, and 50 percent received over 51 percent financial help with the purchase of property.

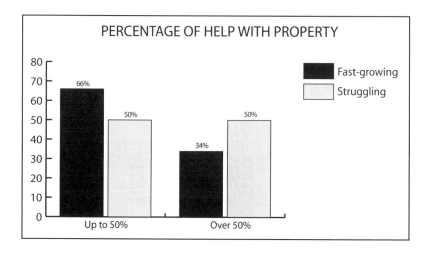

While a 16 percent difference appears between these two groups, the sample is statistically too small to qualify this finding as significant. With only 10 percent of either group reporting they received help purchasing property it would be presumptuous to call this finding significant.

Prayer Networks

Prayer is an important part of any spiritual endeavor. In fact, prayer is often one thing planters do not pay enough attention to. Why? Planters are typically type A, aggressive, entrepreneurial, driven individuals. They get so busy "doing," they often forget to spend time with God. It's not intentional; it's more an issue of personality. But storming the territory of the enemy, is an impossible task without calling upon the power of God through prayer.

Planters were asked if they had built prayer networks that would pray for this new work. I was pleased to see such a high percentage of planters from both groups (65 percent of fast-growing and 64.4 percent of struggling) that responded with a resounding "Yes."

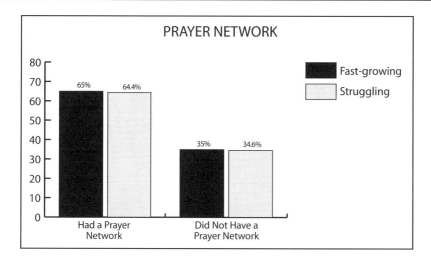

I would love to have tested a few other spiritual markers of participating church planters, but that could take up an entire study all by itself. Besides, finding a way to test spiritual disciplines in an objective way is not an easy task. So, I simply asked one question that I felt would show a small slice of a church planter's spiritual disposition.

Rating of Training

Of those planters who received training, I asked them to rate the training they received. Planters could rate the training as poor, fair, good, very good, and excellent. It was interesting to see that both groups rated their training almost the same.

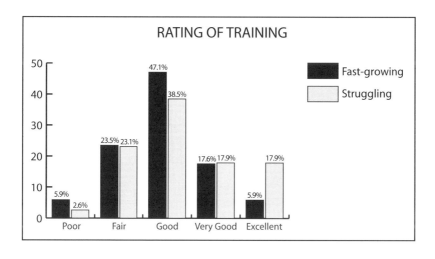

Church Planting Coach

I believe every church planter needs a coach. A good coach will help the planter stay on task by helping him or her find their way through a myriad of issues. Each planter was asked if a coach was provided by the sponsoring agency. No significant differences were discovered between fast-growing and struggling church plants.

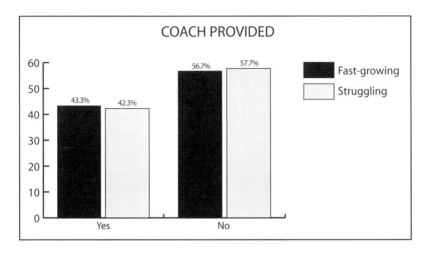

I was very surprised by the lack of coaching being provided for the church planters involved in this study. I expected a much higher return on this question. Only 56.7 percent of fast-growing church planters and 57.7 percent of struggling church planters had a coach. Even though this was not a significant discovery, I think the power of a coach should not be underestimated.

Facility Permanence

Finally, I was very interested to find out if a church plant that started in a permanent facility had an advantage over one that had to rent a space and set up every week. I have often wondered if a permanent facility offers a church plant a sense of credibility in the community. Credibility is vital in a community with so many established churches. So, planters were asked if the place where weekly worship services were held was a place of permanent residence or if they had to set up the facility every week.

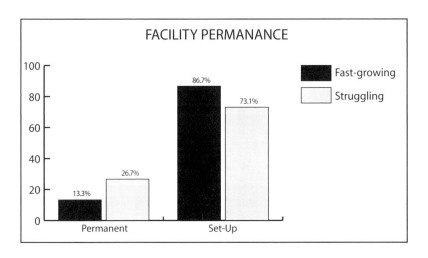

While no significant differences were revealed through this question, struggling church plants did have a higher rate of permanent facility usage. The most important issue coming out of this finding was the fact that an overwhelming percentage of both groups (86.7 percent of fast-growing and 73.1 percent of struggling) used a rented facility in which they had to set up every week. It's important to keep that in mind because renting out a space for a permanent setting can be much more expensive and a new church needs to use money wisely.

A Note on Self-support

The goal of every church plant should be self-support. As a parent desires their children to grow up and make a living on their on, so every mother church or sponsoring agency wishes a new church to grow up and pay its own way. Unfortunately, I have heard too many horror stories about denominations supporting church plants for more than 15 years.

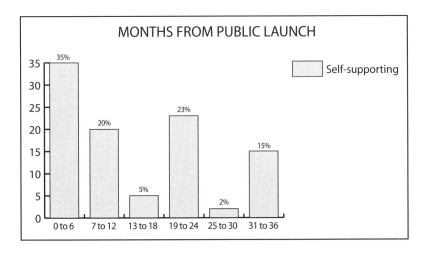

Interestingly, 35 percent of fast-growing church plants were self-support-ing within the first six months from the day of public launch. An additional 20 percent became self-supporting by the end of the first year, 5 percent by eighteen months, and 23 percent by the end of the second year. Here is another point of interest. A total of 83 percent fast-growing church plants reached self-support by the end of the second year.

For more information contact:

Stephen Gray

573-718-3342

Fastgrowingchurchplants@yahoo.com

Church Planting
QUESTIONNAIRE

PLEASE READ EACH QUESTION CAREFULLY and answer it to the best of your ability. Please be as specific as you can on any follow-up questions. If you have any remarks not covered by a question write them beside the question your remark is addressing. Please make sure that the church-planting pastor fills out this questionnaire. All info will be keep confidential.

Biographical Info

Church Name: _____   Date:_____

1. Did you start the church?
   ❏ Yes
   ❏ No

2. Have you started any other churches?
   ❏ Yes
   ❏ No

3. What year was your public launch? _____

4. How many currently attend your weekend services?_____

   If your average attendance is 200 or higher, how many months into the public launch did you reach 200? _____

5. Is the church financially self-supporting?
   ❏ Yes
   ❏ No

   If yes, how many months after public launch did you achieve this? _____

I. SPONSORING AGENCY SUPPORT

(Denomination, Mother church, Association, District)

Finances

These questions were designed to help give clarity to the financial support the planter and plant received. Circle the answer that best applies and answer any follow-up questions that apply.

6. Did you start as a full-time church planter or bi-vocational?
   ❏ Full-time
   ❏ Bi-vocational

7. Did you receive a salary by the sponsoring agent?
   ❏ Full
   ❏ Partial
   ❏ None

   How many years?

   1   2   3   4   5+

8. Did the sponsoring agency provide finances for the purchase of property?
   ❏ Yes
   ❏ No

   What percentage of total property cost did they provide? _____

9. Were you given any additional start-up money by the sponsoring agent?
   ❏ Yes
   ❏ No

   If yes, how much?_____
   ❏ $1,000 - $10,000
   ❏ $10,001 - $25,000
   ❏ $25,001 - $50,000
   ❏ $50,001 - $100,000
   ❏ Over $100,000

10. Did you have to raise any additional finances personally prior to public launch?
   - ❏ Yes
   - ❏ No

Conceptual Freedom

The next six questions were designed to discover the freedom each planter or team had in determining the development of the church plant. Did the sponsoring agency have control or the planter/team? The answers range from 1 to 5, 1 indicating sponsoring agency control and 5 indicating church planter control. Please read the text under each set of numbers and circle the number that best applies.

How much input did you have in the following areas?

11. In creating the vision for the church?

1------------- 2 -------------- 3 -------------- 4 ------------- 5

Sponsoring Agent Control   Shared Control   Planter Control

12. In determining style of worship?

1------------- 2 -------------- 3 -------------- 4 ------------- 5

Sponsoring Agent Control   Shared Control   Planter Control

13. In hiring your own support staff?

1------------- 2 -------------- 3 -------------- 4 ------------- 5

Sponsoring Agent Control   Shared Control   Planter Control

14. In determining where the church was planted?

1------------- 2 -------------- 3 -------------- 4 ------------- 5

Sponsoring Agent Control   Shared Control   Planter Control

15. In determining your target audience?

1------------- 2 -------------- 3 -------------- 4 ------------- 5

Sponsoring Agent Control   Shared Control   Planter Control

16. In determining how the funding was spent?

1------------- 2 -------------- 3 -------------- 4 ------------- 5

Sponsoring Agent Control   Shared Control   Planter Control

Personal Support

This section was designed to discover how much of a role emotional support played in the life of a church plant. Each question has a range from 1 to 5, 1 indicating low levels of support and 5 indicating high levels of support. Please read the text under each set of numbers and circle the number that best applies.

17. How much encouragement did you receive from your superiors?

1------------- 2 -------------- 3 -------------- 4 ------------- 5

Little Encouragement   Moderate Encouragement   High Encouragement

18. How well did you feel you were supported by your pastoral colleagues?

1------------- 2 -------------- 3 -------------- 4 ------------- 5

Low Support   Moderate Support   High Support

19. How well were you accepted by surrounding churches in your denomination?

1------------- 2 -------------- 3 -------------- 4 ------------- 5

Low Acceptance   Moderate Acceptance   High Acceptance

20. Did you have regular fellowship with other pastors?

1------------- 2 -------------- 3 -------------- 4 ------------- 5

Little Fellowship   Moderate Fellowship   High Fellowship

21. Was your work celebrated within the denomination?

1------------- 2 -------------- 3 -------------- 4 ------------- 5

Low Celebration   Moderate Celebration   High Celebration

22. How much negativity did you have to overcome from your sponsoring agency?

1------------- 2 -------------- 3 -------------- 4 ------------- 5

High Negativity   Moderate Negativity   Low Negativity

23. Did you have a prayer network?
❏ Yes
❏ No

Training

This section of the questionnaire addresses the issue of training and assessment. Your answer will give understanding of the role proper training and assessment had on the growth of the church plant. Circle the answer that best applies and answer any follow-up questions that apply.

24. Have you taken the Ridley Assessment?
❏ Yes
❏ No

If yes, would you be willing to share your score?   Score: _____

25. Was specific church-planting training provided for you?
❏ Yes
❏ No

If yes, how much?
❏ Less than 1 week
❏ 1 week
❏ 2 weeks or more

26. How would you rate your training?
    ❏ Poor
    ❏ Fair
    ❏ Good
    ❏ Very Good
    ❏ Excellent
    ❏ N/A

27. Was a church-planting coach provided by the sponsoring agency?
    ❏ Yes
    ❏ No

II. METHODS

Group Development

This section addresses the building of the core group in the development of the church plant. Circle the answer that best applies and answer any follow-up questions that apply.

28. Which model best describes the launch of your church plant?
    ❏ Mother/Daughter
    ❏ Parachute Drop
    ❏ Other
        explain: _____

29. Did this church plant start with a church-planting team or with an individual church planter?
    ❏ Team
    ❏ Individual

    How many paid staff did you start with? (including planter) _____

    How many volunteer staff did you start with? _____

30. How many were in your "core group" before public launch?
    ❏ 1-25
    ❏ 26-50
    ❏ 51-75
    ❏ 76-99
    ❏ Over 100

31. What percentage of your core group were "seed" families from other churches? _____

32. Did you use a "preview service" or small group studies as your main avenue to build your core group?
   ❏ Preview Service
   ❏ Small Groups
   ❏ Both

   If you used preview services, how many did you have prior to public launch?_____

33. How many attended the public launch service?
   ❏ 1-50
   ❏ 51-100
   ❏ 101-150
   ❏ 151-200
   ❏ 201-250
   ❏ Over 250

Strategic Development

This final section was designed to discover the strategies each planter used to develop the church plant. Circle the answer that best applies and answer any follow-up questions that apply.

34. Check the ministries you had in place at the public launch.
   ❏ Worship
   ❏ Children's
   ❏ Teens
   ❏ Singles
   ❏ Men's
   ❏ Women's
   ❏ Senior adults
   ❏ Other _____

35. Which style of worship did you use?
   ❏ Liturgical
   ❏ Traditional
   ❏ Contemporary
   ❏ Blended
   ❏ Postmodern
   ❏ Other _____

36. What type of facility did you use?
   ❏ School
   ❏ Theater
   ❏ Hotel
   ❏ Community Center
   ❏ Home
   ❏ Store front
   ❏ Church
   ❏ Other _____

37. At the time of public launch was the place you worshiped a place of permanent residence or did you set up every week?
   ❏ Permanent
   ❏ Weekly set-up

38. Did you teach financial stewardship in the first six months after public launch?
   ❏ Yes
   ❏ No

39. What percentage of your first year's monthly budget was used for missions and outreach?
   ❏ 0 to 4%
   ❏ 5 to 9%
   ❏ 10% and above

40. Based on your experience, what are the most critical factors that contribute to the fast or slow growth-rate of a church plant?

   _____

   _____

   _____

   _____

Bibliography

Chapter 2

[1]Jones, Tom., et al. *Planting Churches from the Ground Up*. (Joplin, MO: College, 2004), 10.

[2]Malphurs, Aubrey. *Planting Growing Churches for the 21st Century*. (Grand Rapids: Baker, 2000), 42.

[3]Stetzer, Ed. Phone interview. *Planting Missional Churches*. (Nashville: Broadman, 2006), 47.

[4]Gutzke, Manford George. *Plain Talk on Acts*. (Grand Rapids: Zondervan, 1976), 81.

[5]David Olsen. *www.theamericanchurch.org*

[6]Assocation of Religion Data Archives. *Evangelical Deonominations*. Total congregations. *www.thearda.com*

Chapter 3

[1]Sjogren, Steve. *Community of Kindness: A Refreshing New Approach to Planting and Growing a Church*. (Ventura, CA: Regal, 2003), 169.

[2]Wagner, Peter C. *Church Planting for a Greater Harvest*. (Ventura, CA: Regal, 1990), 128.

[3]McIntosh, Gary L. *One Size Doesn't Fit All: Bringing Out the Best in Any Size Church*. (Grand Rapids: Revel, 2005), 17.

[4]Wagner, C. Peter. *Your Church Can Grow*. (Ventura, CA: Regal, 1980), 86.

[5]George, Carl F., and Warren Bird. *How to Break Growth Barriers: Capturing Overlooked Opportunities for Church Growth*. (Grand Rapids: Baker Books, 1993), 138.

[6]Gladwell, Malcom. *The Tipping Point*. (New York: Little, Brown, 2002), 173.

[7]Ibid., 173.

[8]Schaller, Lyle. *Looking in the Mirror*. (Nashville: Abingdon, 1984), 20.

[9]*"Churches Die With Dignity."* Christianity Today (14 Jan. 1991), 36.

[10]McIntosh, Gary L. *One Size Doesn't Fit All: Bringing Out the Best in Any Size Church*. (Grand Rapids: Revel, 2005), 131.

[11]Schaller, Lyle. *Growing Plans: Strategies to Increase Your Church's Membership*. (Nashville: Abingdon, 1989), 21.

Chapter 4

[1]Keener, Ronald E. *"Interview with Ray Johnston."* The Church Executive. (Feb. 2006), 37-42.

[2]Barna, George. *Turn-Around Churches.* (Ventura, CA: Regal Books, 1993), 17.

[3]Collins, Jim. *Good to Great.* (New York: Harper, 2001), 1.

[4]Rainer, Thom S. *Breakout Churches.* (Grand Rapids: Zondervan, 2005),15.

Chapter 5

[1]Maxwell, John. *The 21 Irrefutable Laws of Leadership.* (Thomas Nelson: Nashville, 1998), 1.

[2]Ridley, Charles. *The Church Planter's Assessment Guide.* (Saint Charles, IL: ChurchSmart Resources, 2002), 1-32.

[3]Collins, Jim. *Good to Great.* (New York: Harper, 2001), 13.

Chapter 6

[1]Boan, Rudee Devon. *"Southern Baptist Church-Type Missions: Origin, Development and Outcome, 1979-1984."* (Diss. Southern Baptist Theological Seminary, 1985), 143.

[1]Powell, Dennis D. *"Church-planting Programs of Similar-Sized Denominations in the United States."* (Diss. Asbury Theological Seminary, 2000), 55.

[3]Ibid., 59.

[4]Stetzer, Ed. *Planting Missional Churches.* (Nashville: Broadman, 2006), 221.

Chapter 7

[1]Sweet, Leonard. *Aqua Church: Essential Leadership Arts for Piloting Your Church in Today's Fluid Culture.* (Loveland, CO: Group, 1999), 216.

[2]McLaren, Brian. *The Church on the Other Side.* (Grand Rapids: Zondervan, 2000), 87.

[3]Stevenson, Phil. *The Ripple Church.* (Indianapolis: Wesleyan, 2004), 140.

[1]Schaller, Lyle. *44 Questions for Church Planters.* (Nashville: Abingdon, 1991), 169-72.

[5]Mannioa, Kevin. *Church-planting: The Next Generation.* (Indianapolis: Light and Life, 1994), 59.

[6]Boan, Rudee Devon. *"Southern Baptist Church-Type Missions: Origin, Development and Outcome, 1979-1984."* (Diss. Southern Baptist Theological Seminary, 1985), 92.

Chapter 8

[1]Philippians 3:5-6 (ESV).

[2]Roller, John. *"Advent Christian Church-planting Efforts."* Henceforth: Journal for Advent Christian Thought 8.1 (Fall 1984), 12.

[3]Ibid.,

[4]McCrary, Larry. *"More Than Money."* (Diss. Trinity International, 2001), 65.

Chapter 9

[1]North American Mission Board. *An Analysis of Church-planting Process and Other Selected Factors on the Attendance of Southern Baptist Church Plants: A NAMB Self Study.* (Edward J. Stetzer. 2003), 3.

Chapter 10

[1]Sjogren, Steve. *Community of Kindness: A Refreshing New Approach to Planting and Growing a Church.* (Ventura, CA: Regal, 2003), 110.

[2]Stetzer, Ed. *Planting Missional Churches.* (Nashville: Broadman, 2006), 71.

Chapter 11

[1]Wagner, C. Peter. *Church Planting for a Greater Harvest.* (Ventura, CA: Regal, 1990), 120

[2]Bulley, Gary. *An Introduction to Church-planting-Part 3, Developing a Contextualized Church-planting Strategy*, 34.

[3]Powell, Dennis D. *"Church-planting Programs of Similar-Sized Denominations in the United States."* (Diss. Asbury Theological Seminary, 2000), 54.

[4]Schaller, Lyle. *44 Questions for Church Planters.* (Nashville: Abingdon, 1991), 67.

[5]Schaller, Lyle. *Growing Plans: Strategies to Increase Your Church's Membership.* (Nashville: Abingdon, 1989), 21.

Chapter 12

[1]Sjogren, Steve. *Community of Kindness: A Refreshing New Approach to Planting and Growing a Church.* (Ventura, CA: Regal, 2003), 78.

[2]Warren, Rick. *The Purpose Driven Church.* (Grand Rapids: Zondervan, 1995), 90.

[3]North American Mission Board. *An Analysis of Church-planting Process and Other Selected Factors on the Attendance of Southern Baptist Church Plants: A NAMB Self Study.* Edward J. Stetzer. (2003), 9.

[4]Schaller, Lyle. *44 Questions for Church Planters.* (Nashville: Abingdon, 1991), 61.

[5]North American Mission Board. *An Analysis of Church-planting Process and Other Selected Factors on the Attendance of Southern Baptist Church Plants: A NAMB Self Study.* (Edward J. Stetzer), 10.

[6]Powell, Dennis D. *"Church-planting Programs of Similar-Sized Denominations in the United States."* (Diss. Asbury Theological Seminary, 2000), 83.